Norman P. Lieske
Michael Losse

Die schönsten Schlösser,
Villen und Palais in und um

MÜNCHEN

Wartberg Verlag

Über München sind vom Wartberg Verlag erhältlich:

(1) München – Bewegte Zeiten – Die 50er Jahre
(2) Kindheit in München in den 50er Jahren
(3) Das Millionendorf – Münchner Geschichten aus den 50er Jahren
(4) Hurra, wir leben noch! – München nach 1945
(5) Wir Kriegskinder – Münchner Zeitzeugen erinnern sich
(6) Die schönsten Schlösser, Villen und Palais in und um München

Bildnachweis:

Alle Fotos von Norman P. Lieske

Textnachweis:

Die deutschen Texte stammen von Michael Losse, mit Ausnahme des Textes über das Palais Gise, das Hofmarkschloss Planegg und die Stadtresidenz Preysing von Norman P. Lieske.

Die deutschen Texte von Michael Losse wurden vom Wartberg Verlag überarbeitet.

Die englischen Texte stammen von Norman P. Lieske.

Die englischen Übersetzungen geben die deutschen Texte nicht wort-, wohl aber inhaltsgetreu wieder.

1. Auflage 2005

Druck: Bernecker, Melsungen

Buchbinderische Verarbeitung: Büge, Celle

34281 Gudensberg-Gleichen

Im Wiesental 1

Tel.: 05603/93050

www.wartberg-verlag.de

ISBN 3-8313-1504-3

Inhaltsverzeichnis | Contents

Fürstliche Residenzen und Schlösser

The Royal Palaces and Castles

Stadtpalais des mittleren Adels

The Town Palaces of the Noble Families

Die berühmten Villen

The Famous Villas

Burgen und Schlösser in der Umgebung

The Castles around Munich

Legende
Altes Schloss
Schloss, Villa, Palais
Castle, villa, palais
A 8
Autobahn
Motorway
Mehrspurige Fernverkehrsstraße
Multilane arterial road
Fernverkehrsstraße
Arterial road
Sonstige Straße
Other road
Eisenbahnlinie
Railway
Fluss, See
River, lake
Bebauung
City, town, village
Flughafen
Airport
0 2 4 km
N
W
O
S
Moosburg
Amper
Isar
Zolling
Langenbach
A 9
Allershausen
Freising
Kranzberg
Domburg/Residenz
Amper
A 92
Flughafen München
Erding
Stadtburg
Hallbergmoos
Haimhausen
Neufahrn
· Schloss Nymphenburg mit
· Parkschloss Amalienburg,
· Parkschloss Badenburg,
· Parkschloss Magdalenenklause,
· Parkschloss Pagodenburg
Eching
Unterschleißheim
Dachau
A 92
Neues Schloss
Schloss Dachau
Altes Schloss
Schloss Lustheim
Garching
Ismaning
Schloss Ismaning
Mittlerer Isarkanal
Amper
A 8
Oberschleißheim
Karlsfeld
A 99
Isar
Speichersee
Feldmoching
A 9
Markt Schwaben
Olching
A 8
A 99
München
Gröbenzell
Moosach
Poing
Obermenzing
Schwabing
Kirchheim
A 94
Eichenau
Prinz-Carl-Palais
Anzing
Schloss Blutenburg
Nymphenburg
Villa Lenbach
Bogenhausen
Feldkirchen
Puchheim
Stuck-Villa
A 94
Pasing
Hbf.
A 99
Germering
A 96
Giesing
Vaterstetten
Gräfelfing
Haar
Zorneding
A 96
Planegg
Asam-Schlößl
Perlach
Hofmarkschloss
Kirchseeon
Neuried
Thalkirchen
A 8
Neubiberg
Krailing
A 995
Unterhaching
Ottobrunn
Gauting
Pullach
Burg Schwaneck
A 99
Würm
A 95
Taufkirchen
Burg Grünwald
· Alter Hof
· Residenz
· Arco-Palais
· Marstall (Alte Münze)
· Palais Holnstein
· Leuchtenberg Palais
· Palais Ludwig-Ferdinand
· Palais Portia
· Palais des Grafen Preysing
· Palais Törring (Hauptpost)
· Palais Gise
· Palais Preysing
Starnberg
Isar
Oberhaching
Höhenkirchen-Siegertsbrunn
A 952
Schäftlarn
Sauerlach
Aying
A 95
Starnberger See
A 8
Feldkirchen
Wolfratshausen

Alter Hof

Etwa zwischen Frauenkirche und Hofbräuhaus, nur wenige Minuten zu Fuß vom Marienplatz, befindet sich der Alte Hof, die ältere der zwei Wittelsbacher Burgen in München. Nachdem Ludwig der Strenge bei der bayerischen Landesteilung 1255 Oberbayern und die Rheinpfalz erhalten hatte, nahm er seinen Sitz in München.

Vor Ort

Gönnen Sie sich eine zünftige Brotzeit im Hofbräuhaus oder einer anderen der zahlreichen Gaststätten dieser Gegend, um sich dann frisch gestärkt auf den Weg zum Alten Hof zu machen. Nach wenigen Schritten taucht er vor Ihnen auf und präsentiert sich in mittelalterlichen Formen und Farben. Gehen Sie von dort aus weiter in Richtung Maximilianstraße, erreichen Sie schnell den Max-Joseph-Platz und blicken auf den südlichen Teil der Residenz und das Palais Törring gegenüber.

Informationen zur Geschichte und Architektur

Die Burg wurde mehrfach verändert und erweitert. Ab 1466 wurden der Zwingerstock und der Burgstock (Südflügel, im 20. Jh. Finanzamt) mit dem Affentürmchen, einem dreigeschossigen hölzernen Erker, umgestaltet. Über diesen Turmerker dichtete Thomas Greidl aus Steinfelden: „Nun ist aber ein Turm darunter / An dem kann man sehen ein Wunder / Den Meister soll man billig loben, / Spitzig ist er [der Erker] unten und oben, / Rührt weder Himmel noch Erde an, / Tat dennoch unbeweglich stahn."

Nachdem es ab 1384/85 Konflikte zwischen dem Herzog und der Münchner Bürgerschaft gab und die Burg durch die Ausdehnung der Stadtbefestigung in Richtung Norden die Stadtrandlage eingebüßt hatte, wurde ab 1385 eine neue Burg an der Nordostseite der Stadt erbaut. Der Alte Hof bestand weiter.

Nach Zerstörungen im Zweiten Weltkrieg wurde die Burg teils neu aufgebaut und der vorherige Charakter der Vierflügelanlage annähernd wieder gewonnen.

Insgesamt umfasst der Burgkomplex Bausubstanz des 13./14.–16. Jahrhunderts. Ein zweischiffiger kreuzgewölbter Keller mit Bandrippen ist besonders zu erwähnen, ebenso Teile des Dachwerks aus dem 15. und 16. Jahrhundert.

Ausstattungsstücke der Burg befinden sich im Bayerischen Nationalmuseum.

Information

Burgstaße 8, München. Der Burghof ist frei zugänglich.
Verkehrsanbindung:
S-Bahnlinien 1-8 oder U-Bahnlinien 3/6 bis Marienplatz.

Just 5 minutes walk north from Marienplatz, this very first spot of the 1158 founded settlement of Munich, is the "Alter Hof" (Old Court), the oldest of the two Wittelsbach castles in this town.

When in 1240 the Wittelsbach family were appointed Dukes of Bavaria-Munich, this facility became their royal seat. For more than 700 years, the Wittelsbach family ruled Bavaria as Dukes, Electors and finally Kings.

Up today this building complex has well preserved its medieval appearance.

Your Sightseeing

Sunday morning you might have a breakfast in one of the restaurants bordering the "Platzl". The best known is the "Hofbräuhaus", but there are others offering different styles. One short street and only a few steps away, you find the "Alter Hof". Around high noon, the main building appears at glancing incidence of the sunlight. Enjoy the impression of real medieval shapes and of delicate colours.

From there emerge onto the Maximilianstreet and head for the stately Max-Joseph-Platz bordered on three sides with the southern front of the residence and the "Palais Törring" opposite to it.

Information about history and architecture

It has not been finally clarified if the first Duke Ludwig der Strenge (the stringent) in 1255 started with a new building or if he merely rebuilt an older one. In the years ahead the castle was rebuilt and extended several times. Ludwig IV, duke since 1302, 1314 king and 1328-1347 emperor of the ancient German Reich, had built the large hall on the western side of the complex. In 1466 Duke Sigismund commissioned to redesign the southern wing, part of it the prominent three-tiered wooden turret.

Towards the end of the 14th century conflicts emerging between the Duke and the Munich citizens as well as the ongoing northward extension of the town's fortifications, let the Duke build a new castle. This "Neuveste" later merged into the "Royal Residence".

The "Old Court" complex as you see it nowadays, includes building structures dating from the 13th-16th century.

Numerous pieces of the old court's furniture are exhibited in the "Bavarian National Museum".

Alter Hof

Herzoglicher Marstall

und Alte Münze

Als Bindeglied zwischen dem Alten Hof und der Neuveste/Residenz – mit beiden Burgen jeweils durch einen gedeckten Gang verbunden – entstand der herzogliche Marstall mit der Kunstkammer im zweiten Obergeschoss 1563/67, während der Amtszeit Herzogs Albrecht V. von Bayern, anstelle dreier Bürgerhäuser. Heute beherbergt der Alte Marstall das Bayerische Landesamt für Denkmalpflege.

Vor Ort

Am besten besuchen Sie den Herzoglichen Marstall in der Woche vormittags. Aber geben Sie Acht: Die äußere, eher schlichte Fassade kann leicht übersehen werden. Betreten Sie das Gebäude durch die hölzerne Haupteingangstür (was nur innerhalb der Woche zu den Bürozeiten möglich ist) und gehen zum Innenhof. Beim Anblick der farbig ausgestalteten, dreistöckigen Renaissance-Arkaden werden Sie sich sogleich ins Mittelalter zurückversetzt fühlen.

Informationen zur Geschichte und Architektur

1807–09 wurde der Bau nach Entwürfen von Andreas Gärtner und Franz Thurn zur königlich-bayerischen Münze umgestaltet. Ein neuer Marstall in Verbindung mit einer Hofreitschule entstand 1817–22 nach Entwürfen von Leo von Klenze östlich der Residenz (Marstallplatz/-straße) als klassizistischer Bau.
Nach verhältnismäßig leichten Beschädigungen im Zweiten Weltkrieg wurde das Gebäude im Innern teils verändert.
Die Außenfassaden des viergeschossigen Gebäudes sind schlicht, doch wirkungsvoll gestaltet und letztlich nur durch die Fensterreihungen gegliedert. Über unregelmäßigem Grundriss errichtet umschließt die Vierflügelanlage des Alten Marstalles einen dreigeschossigen Renaissance-Arkadenhof. Kurze Säulen mit ionisierenden Kapitellen tragen die unteren Arkaden, während die obere Säulenreihe aus Rotmarmor eine toskanische Gestaltung zeigt.
Als kleiner Teil der ehemaligen Stallungen (für Pferde und wohl auch Kühe) im Erdgeschoss blieb die dreischiffige Säulenhalle im Südflügel erhalten. Zum Raumprogramm gehörten darüber hinaus Wagenremisen und Weinkeller sowie in den oberen Geschossen – außer der Kunstkammer, den Räumlichkeiten für die herzoglichen Sammlungen – ein Tanzsaal, eine Kapelle, aufwändig ausgestattete Gemächer der Herzogsfamilie, Personalräume und schließlich der so genannte „Baumgarten“ für Kübelpflanzen.

Information

Hofgraben 4, München
Verkehrsanbindung:
S-Bahnlinien 1-8 oder U-Bahnlinien 3/6 bis Marienplatz.

Very few steps north from the "Old Court" one of the architectural and art historical gems of the Bavarian Capital, the "Royal Stable" – "Old Mint" is seated.. The different names elucidate the different purposes the building was used for during the past ages.
Bearing one of the very few three-story high arcades, it constitutes a major achievement among German secular Renaissance buildings.

Your Sightseeing

You should visit this sight on a weekday morning around 10 to eleven. Take care not to overlook the building due to its unspectacular front appearance from the street. Nowadays it houses the Bavarian State Department of Historical Monuments (Bayerisches Landesamt für Denkmalpflege). You enter the building through the wooden main entrance door (admittance only during weekday business hours), step into the inner courtyard and walk around the three-tiered corridors. You will be hit by the impression of the grandiose Renaissance arcades, their massive pillars revelling in rich blue and pink colours.
Make a pause, standing there completely surrounded by this narrow and massive complex, and you might feel as if taken back to the old ages.

Information about history and architecture

1563 to 67 Duke Albrecht V commissioned the court's master builder Wilhelm Egkl to construct this facility connected to either one of the Wittelsbach castles by hidden passage ways. It was used as a Royal Stable and as a private museum for art objects.
1807 to 09 the building was reconfigured and further used as the Royal Bavarian Mint. It served this purpose until 1983, finally as part of the German Bundesbank.
Nowadays it houses the "Bayerisches Landesamt für Denkmalpflege".
The four wing building complex surrounds an irregular trapezoid inner yard, the three-tiered Renaissance arcades of which in terms of art history are quite high up the list of Renaissance buildings within Europe.
Short massive pillars with ionic capitals support the two lower arcades, whereas the upper arcade is made up of slender Tuscan columns built from red marble stone.

Herzoglicher Marstall

Residenz mit Innenhöfen Innenräumen und Hofgärten

Vor Ort

Wenn Sie den gesamten Gebäudekomplex erkunden möchten, sollten Sie sich einen ganzen Tag Zeit nehmen. So gewinnen Sie einen umfassenden Einblick in eine längst vergangene Zeit mit ihrer monumentalen Architektur, bedeutenden Kunstwerken und einer einladenden Gartenlandschaft.

Informationen zur Geschichte und Architektur

Aus der neuen Burg (Neuveste) der Wittelsbacher hervorgegangen, war die Residenz als Regierungssitz vom Spätmittelalter bis 1918 das politische, künstlerische und kulturelle Zentrum Bayerns, anfangs des Herzogtums, dann des Kurfürstentums und des Königreichs Bayern (1806–1918). Viele der Herrscher ließen den Komplex nach Entwürfen bedeutender Künstler und Architekten umgestalten und erweitern. Hier waren ihre Kunstsammlungen und der Hausschatz untergebracht.

Neuveste

Durch die Ausdehnung der Stadtbefestigung nach Norden stand die einst an deren Rand gelegene Herzogsburg im 14. Jahrhundert inmitten der Stadt. Nachdem es aber ab 1384/85 zu Auseinandersetzungen zwischen dem Herzog und der Münchner Bürgerschaft gekommen war, schien die Verlegung der Burg geboten. 1385 begann der Bau der Neuveste an der Nordostseite der Stadt. Mehrfach erweitert, wurde sie zu einer unregelmäßigen vierflügeligen Wasserburg mit Türmen an drei Ecken und hatte um 1570 ihre größte Ausdehnung erreicht.
Wenig blieb von jenem aus historischen Abbildungen bekannten Schloss der Spätgotik und Renaissance, doch sind im Hofpflaster markierte Fundamente unter dem Apothekerhof der Residenz erhalten. Mit dem Bau des Antiquariums 1569–71 von Hofbaumeister Wilhelm Egkl für die Kunst- und Antikensammlung unter Herzog Albrecht V. südwestlich der Burg begann die über den Bereich der Neuveste hinausgehende Bebauung. Nach und nach entstanden Neubauten westlich und südlich der Burg, die vorerst noch erhalten blieb, schließlich aber dem Festsaalbau (1832-42) zum Opfer fiel.

Located between the stately but somehow narrow Max-Joseph-Platz, which emerges into the famous Maximilian street, and the more spacious Odeonsplatz leading into the classical Ludwig street, piles up the "Residence", the Royal Palace of the Wittelsbach family. From here they ruled Bavaria over 500 years from 1385 to 1918 as Dukes, Princes, Electors and Kings.
The Palace constitutes one of the outstanding European Renaissance buildings. The present Residence, severely damaged during the last war and almost completely rebuilt until 1980, dates from the 16th century. Essential parts have been added in the Baroque and Rococo style during the 18th century and in the classical style during the 19th century.
Besides the building, the complex includes 5 major inner courtyards as well as the magnificent Residence garden.
The building itself houses the "Residence Museum", the "Residence Treasury", the "Old Residence Theatre" and finally the "Egyptian Museum".
Highlights are the spectacular Renaissance Hall "Antiquarium", the Old Theatre named after its creator "Cuvilliés Theater" - easily the world's most famous Rococo theatre - and the more than hundred resplendent showrooms with plenty of exquisite art objects.

Your Sightseeing

As with every sight you might step in nearly at any time to have a short look.
However, if you take a whole day and make a real visit to the entire complex, you will be definitely rewarded. Rewarded with the total impression of an ancient world, closed off the outside and made up of a monumental architecture, significant art pieces and a comforting garden landscape.
The different parts, buildings - courtyards - garden, need different day times set for a visit:
In the early morning hours, you stroll through the Residence Garden.
In the late morning to noontime you might linger in the courtyards area, enjoying the best light for the diverse architecture.
The whole afternoon you would like to spend inside the buildings: The showrooms of the "Residence Museum" are filled with grandiose furnishings, superb paintings and extravagant pieces of silver and porcelain.
The "Residence Treasury", 1565 founded by Duke Albrecht V (by testimony he declared all present and future collection pieces as unsaleable) lays out unique and exquisite works of jewellery, crystal, tableware, the crown insignia as well as ancient religious pieces.

Residenz

RESIDENZ
MUNCHEN
RESIDENZ
MUSEUM

*Max-Joseph-Platz
mit Blick auf die Residenz*

Residenz

Nach dem Bau des Antiquariums entstand, nach dem Brand in der Neuveste 1580, unter Herzog Wilhelm V. (reg. 1579–97) 1580/81 der zweigeschossige Witwenbau an der vorderen Schwabinger Gasse, in deren Richtung die Residenz nun weiter wuchs. Es folgten ab 1581 der Neue Gartenbau (von Friedrich Sustris) westlich neben dem Antiquarium, der den Grottenhof umschließt, und der Erbprinzentrakt.
Nachdem der Neuveste immer neue Bauten hinzugefügt worden waren, begann Herzog Maximilian I. (reg. 1597–1651) in den 1610er Jahren mit der Vereinheitlichung des Residenzbaues, wozu er kurz zuvor errichtete Bauten an der Schwabinger Gasse abbrechen und einen symmetrischen zweigeschossigen Vierflügelbau mit Mezzanin nördlich des Jägergassls bauen ließ, der die Bauten am Brunnen-, Grotten- und Kapellenhof zusammenfügte und insgesamt fünf Höfe umschloss. Auch der Hofgarten und die neue Stadtbefestigung (Bastionärbefestigung) entstanden unter Maximilian I.
Nachdem Bayern 1806 ein Königreich geworden war, bestand der Wunsch nach neuen repräsentativen Bauten im Bereich der Residenz. So entstanden 1812–42 das Hof- und Nationaltheater und die Bauten, die Leo v. Klenze entwarf: die neue Reitschule anstelle der Zeughäuser im Osten, die Allerheiligen-Hofkirche, der Königsbau für König Ludwig I. und der Festsaalbau am Hofgarten.
Im Zweiten Weltkrieg wurde die Residenz stark zerstört, doch schon bald nach dem Krieg in Teilen neu aufgebaut. Heute zählt das Museum in der Residenz zu den bedeutendsten Raumkunst-Museen Europas.

Innenhöfe

Im Nordwesten befindet sich der Kaiserhof, südlich davon der Kapellenhof sowie der Grottenhof (mit seiner künstlichen Grotte) und der Königsbauhof. Im östlichen Teil des Residenzkomplexes liegen der Apothekenhof, der Brunnenhof und der Küchenhof.

Innenräume und Cuvilliéstheater

Zu den zu besichtigenden Bereichen innerhalb des Residenzkomplexes gehören das Residenzmuseum – es umfasst fürstliche Räume der Renaissance, des Rokoko und des Klassizismus –, das Alte Residenztheater (sog. Cuvilliéstheater) und die Schatzkammer, in der Kronen, Goldschmiedekunst etc. von der Spätantike bis zum Klassizismus präsentiert werden. Sammlungen und historische Prunkräume wurden 1920 für Besucher geöffnet.
Einer der bemerkenswertesten Innenräume ist das Antiquarium, das die Antikensammlung Herzogs Albrecht V. aufnehmen sollte. Der tonnengewölbte Renaissance-Saal zeigt Groteskenmalereien und Ansichten bayerischer Burgen, Schlösser, Städte und Märkte.
1750 kam es zu einem Großbrand in der Residenz, bei dem der als Theater genutzte Georgssaal zerstört wurde. Kur-

In the "Egyptian Museum" impressive statues and other cultural works from the old, classical and late period of the ancient Egypt kingdom are gripping your attention.
After having seen so many spectacular works, you should recuperate and recover your senses by staying for a short while within the Antiquarium. This largest secular Renaissance hall north of the Alps has been built 1571 for housing Duke Albrecht's collection of antique sculptures and his library. Later used for festivals, it still nowadays plays host for official events and receptions. Its especial side daylight illumination and the vaulted ceilings covered with superb paintings might give you a real breathtaking impression.
The best way to appreciate the lavishly decorated Rococo style "Cuvielliés Theatre" is to visit an evening performance.
For your breakfast, lunch and dinner you have a choice between numerous different style restaurants and bistros placed around the Josephplatz, on the west front of the Residence building or even inside on the Kaiserhof.

Information about history and architecture

In 1385, the Duke initialised the construction of the new castle "Neuveste". Several extensions during the 15th and 16th century resulted in an irregular 4-wing castle surrounded by water and with towers on three corners.
A new array of buildings appeared to the west and south of the "Neuveste", starting with the construction of the "Antiquarium" from 1569–71 under the rule of Duke Albrecht V. By the time, the whole complex became the "Residence Palace".
From 1610 on Duke Maximilian I cared for a reconfiguration of the Residence buildings. He commissioned a symmetric 4-wing complex with two storeys and a mezzanine floor, and enclosing 5 major courtyards. The front exteriors facing the courtyards and the streets respectively were painted with fictitious architectural structures.
Duke Maximilian I also had built the Residence Garden and the town's fortifications between 1619–38.
In 1751 Prince Elector Max III Joseph commissioned François de Cuvilliés the Elder to build the "Old Residence Theatre" just south of the Residence Garden. This in terms of art history extremely significant work was finished in 1755. The renowned artists Johann Baptist Straub and Johann Baptist Zimmermann have made major contributions to the furnishings.
When in 1806 Bavaria was granted to become a kingdom, new representative buildings were commissioned. It was Leo von Klenze, a major architect of German classicism, who built the court church in 1826, the "Königsbau", the façade of wich appeals to the famous Palazzo Pitti of Florence, for King Ludwig I in 1835, and in 1842 the festivity hall at the Residence Garden. The latter building was very much modelled on the works of the Italian Renaissance architect Palladio.

Blick auf die Hofgartenseite der Residenz

Residenz, Eingang Odeonsplatz

Blick durch die Viscardigasse auf die Residenz

fürst Max III. Joseph ließ daraufhin ab 1751 das Alte Residenztheater nach Plänen von François de Cuvilliés d. Ä. im Stil des Rokoko als Opernhaus südlich des Hofgartens erbauen.
Mit der Residenz wurde das Theater 1944 zerstört. Die Verkleidungen der Logen waren jedoch rechtzeitig in Sicherheit gebracht worden. So konnte das Theater nach dem Krieg an anderer Stelle, am Brunnenhof, neu aufgebaut und zur 800-Jahr-Feier Münchens 1958 eröffnet werden.

Hofgarten

Der heutige Hofgarten nordnordöstlich der Residenz mit dem Diana-Tempel geht jedoch auf einen Lustgarten Kurfürst Maximilians I. zurück. Dieser kurfürstliche Garten soll „holländische" Buchsbeet- und Zwiebelblumen-Anlagen sowie Laubengänge umfasst haben.
Seit dem 17. Jahrhundert wurde der Hofgarten, der in die frühneuzeitliche Bastionärbefestigung der Stadt einbezogen war, mehrfach verändert: 1776 erfuhr der höher gelegene Bereich eine Umgestaltung zum Baumgarten mit linearen Pflanzungen. Der tiefer liegende Bereich wurde um 1800 zum Exerzierplatz. Die Neugestaltung des Gartens nach dem Zweiten Weltkrieg orientierte sich am Zustand des frühen 17. Jahrhunderts mit Kreuz- und Diagonalwegen, Blumen-, Rasen- und Heckenparterres und Springbrunnen, umgeben von Bäumen.

Information

Max-Joseph-Platz 3, München
Verkehrsanbindung: U-Bahnlinien 3/4/5/6 bis Odeonsplatz.

Residence Garden

The "Residence Garden" is bordering the Residence building complex to the north, is facing the "Odeonsplatz" to the west, and to the east it opens right hand to the Bavarian State Chancellery, left hand to the Prince Carl Palais (see below).
This Italianate court garden is an exceptional spot for recuperation and contemplation.
The garden presents itself laid out geometrically, crossed with parallel and diagonal footpaths, and planted with rich coloured flowers.

Your Sightseeing

If you do not mind to get up very early, you should stroll through this garden in the wee hours of a Sunday morning.
Stepping in from the Odeonsplatz you directly look at the Residence building front with the morning sun in your eyes. This and the morning haze help the pilasters and statuaries of the building to appear mysterious and attractive alike.
At this daytime, it is your garden and you feel tempted to linger in it. There are paths to walk, wooden benches to sit on and to view at one of the fountains with its water splashing down into a stone bowl.
You would like to look closely at the octagonal "Diana Temple", centring the garden and with its dome bearing a bronze statue of the hunting goddess. From inside this temple you will enjoy an exciting view at the "Theatiner" church, their mighty, soaring towers glowing in the direct light of the morning sun.
You find yourself back on earth and feel hungry for breakfast. A few steps south on the Josephplatz you will find restaurants and bistros offering a rich Bavarian breakfast.

Information about history and architecture

The original court garden goes back to the times of Duke Maximilian I and was laid out between 1613 and 1617 as an Italianate Renaissance garden. This ducal pleasance already saw the Diana temple, the arcades bordering the garden to the west and to the north, many flowerbeds and alleys.
In the early 18th century, when the Baroque gardens of Nymphenburg and Schleißheim castles turned out to be of greater importance, just the northern arcades have been extended into a picture gallery.
In the 19th century, it was the first work of the later court architect von Klenze, to renovate the west arcades and to add a classical triumphal arch as a gateway to the Odeonsplatz.

Inner courtyards

The Residence building surrounds five major inner courtyards, the "Kaiserhof" (emperor courtyard), the "Apothekenhof" (pharmacy courtyard), the "Kapellenhof" (chapel courtyard), the "Brunnenhof" (fountain courtyard) and the "Königsbauhof" (king's building courtyard).
They have retained their original appearance and in contrast to the Residence front exterior, which is looming up to the visitor, their architecture creates the impression of safety and order.

Your Sightseeing

Why not to continue your Sunday morning stay in the Residence garden and after having enjoyed your breakfast you might start the exploration of the inner courtyards.
It is the late morning light and the absence of any crowd of tourists, which can transport you back to the old ages. Close your eyes and try to hear the sound of the horse hooves on the cobbled ground, the commands of orderlies or the laughter of the ladies-in-waiting stepping out of the horse carriages … or something like this.
Do not miss to visit the "Brunnenhof" and linger at the enormous "Wittelsbach Fountain", highly impressive with its gorgeous statuaries.
Here is an option: to visit the inner courtyards at dusk time, might definitely be quite a special experience for you. Completely different as now appear the contours and colours of the architecture.

Apothekenhof

Kaiserhof

Blick auf die Residenz

Brunnenhof

Blick in den Hofgarten auf Dianatempel und Theatinerkirche

Schloss Nymphenburg

mit Amalienburg, Badenburg, Pagodenburg und Magdalenenklause

Schloss Nymphenburg liegt eingebettet in eine einzigartige Parklandschaft, zu der vier weitere Lustschlösser innerhalb des weitläufigen Parks gehören. Darüber hinaus ist es eingebunden in eine der umfassendsten europäischen Landschaftsplanungen des Barockzeitalters, die durch Schneisen und Sichtachsen optische Verbindungen zu ausgewählten Punkten herstellte und durch Kanäle die Verbindung zu weiteren Schlössern herstellte. In ganz Europa war dieses Gesamtkunstwerk im 18. Jahrhundert bekannt. Heute gehört Nymphenburg zu den meistbesuchten Schlössern in Deutschland.

Vor Ort

Auch für die Besichtigung der Nymphenburger Schlösser und des Parks sollten Sie sich einen ganzen Tag Zeit nehmen. Legen Sie Ihren Besuch, wenn möglich, innerhalb der Woche, um den Genuss der Besichtigung der Gebäude und Landschaft nicht mit Tausenden teilen zu müssen. Denjenigen, die keinen Picknickkorb dabei haben, sei das Restaurant im Park empfohlen.
Übrigens: Auch für Familien mit Kindern ist die Anlage ein wahres Paradies, können sich doch die Kleinen nach anstrengenden Besichtigungstouren immer wieder im Grünen austoben.
Beginnen Sie Ihren Spaziergang am Nymphenburger Schloss entlang des kleinen Kanals. Nach etwa zehn Minuten erreichen Sie, reizvoll zwischen einer Gruppe von Bäumen gelegen, das Parkschloss Amalienburg. Versäumen Sie nicht, den Spiegelsaal im Innern zu besichtigen. Sie werden sich fühlen wie im Märchenland ...
Wir empfehlen Ihnen, den Spaziergang von der Amalienburg zur Badenburg möglichst auf den späten Nachmittag zu legen. Wenn Sie die Seeseite gegenüber der Badenburg erreichen, bietet sich Ihnen zu dieser Tageszeit ein atemberaubender Blick auf die sich im Wasser spiegelnde Amalienburg. Insbesondere die ihrer Zeit weit vorausgreifende Einrichtung des „Badezimmers" wird Sie begeistern.
Wenn Sie von der Badenburg kommen, müssen Sie nur die Brücke über den Hauptkanal überqueren, um einen kleinen Teich zu erreichen. Auf dessen gegenüberliegender Seite grüßt bereits die Pagodenburg mit ihrer eindrucksvollen Rokokofassade.
Nach der Besichtigung der Innenräume sei eine Pause auf den Bänken vor dem Schloss oder am Teich empfohlen.
Welch ein Kontrast zu den anderen Parkschlössern! Man fühlt sich sogleich ins Mittelalter zurückversetzt, wenn man vor der (künstlichen) Ruine steht – ziemlich unheimlich im Licht der untergehenden Sonne ...

Among all German castles, Nymphenburg is arguably the one with the largest number of visitors.
The breathtaking Baroque palace is surrounded by an extensive and beautiful landscaped park. Embedded into this spacious parkland are four summer residences.
Over water canals and land lanes Nymphenburg castle was connected to other castles. The entire complex as a synthesis of building and landscape was famous during the Baroque ages all over Europe.

Your Sightseeing

You had better a whole day for exploring the Nymphenburg castle and park. Forget the weekend, especially the Sunday, for this adventure, because hundreds of busses transport thousands of tourists into that area.
You might explore the whole facility or just promenade through the park, either way you will spend a very satisfying day.
You should start in the early morning hours (the park is open all day) and walk into that part of the park directly adjacent to the south front of the castle. In the morning haze stroll between fountains and flowerbeds and by the water watch the swans and ducks busy with their morning activities. Find a bench to sit down and enjoy your breakfast coffee and sandwiches.
Now you feel ready to step into the palace building and to explore its highlights: the "Great Hall" - a lavishly decorated Rococo room -, the "Hall of Beauties" - a painting gallery of the most beautiful ladies from Munich of those days -, the "Royal Stable Museum" exhibiting the famous golden carriage and the horse-drawn winter sleigh of the fairytale king Ludwig II. Finally, you should not miss to see the "Porcelain Museum" with its collection of exquisite world famous pieces made by Bustelli.
After having had a lunch break in the park restaurant, you should feel strong enough during the afternoon to explore the four summer residences spread out over the park area.
The Rococo style "Amalienburg" and the brick stone made hermitage "Magdalenenklause" reward you with romantic impressions in the early afternoon light. The "Badenburg" and "Pagodenburg", both seated on small lakes need the late afternoon sunlight to bring out the beautiful details of their façades.

Schloss Nymphenburg

Schloss Nymphenburg

Schloss Nymphenburg

Etwa 7 km von der Münchner Residenz entfernt lag das landwirtschaftliche Anwesen der Schwaige Kemnat (Kemnathen), das Kurfürst Ferdinand Maria anlässlich der Geburt des Thronfolgers Max Emanuel 1662 seiner Gattin Adelaide von Savoyen schenkte, um hier ihr „Castello delle Nymphe“ zu errichten. 1664 begannen die Bauarbeiten. Es entstand der annähernd würfelförmige fünfstöckige Mittelbau des heutigen Schlosses.
Vor der Westseite erstreckte sich ein Gartenparterre mit Wasserbassins und Fontänen. Erst ab 1673 plante Enrico Zuccalli dann den Innenausbau, und bis zum Tod der Bauherrin 1676 blieb das Schloss unvollendet. Ihr Sohn, Kurfürst Max Emanuel, ließ weiterbauen.
Wegen des Spanischen Erbfolgekrieges floh der Kurfürst 1704. Die Bauarbeiten ruhten bis zu seiner Rückkehr 1714. Ab dann entstanden der Orangerietrakt im Norden und der Marstalltrakt (heute Marstallmuseum) im Süden, sodass das Schloss schließlich eine Gesamtlänge von knapp 1,5 km aufwies.
Das so genannte Rondell, zehn im Halbkreis angeordnete Kavaliershäuser östlich des Schlosses, wurde nach 1728 gebaut. Kurfürst Max III. Joseph ließ das Schloss im Stil des Rokoko erneut verändern. Die Umgestaltung des Großen Saales im Mittelbau unter der Leitung von Johann Baptist Zimmermanns und François Cuvilliés d. Ä. erbrachte einen der bemerkenswertesten Innenräume jener Epoche in Deutschland.
Zur Ausstattung des Schlosses gehört die Schönheitsgalerie, eine Sammlung von Porträts schöner Frauen, welche Joseph Stieler im Auftrag König Ludwigs I. von Bayern 1827/50 malte.
Der italienischen Vorbildern folgende Schlossgarten wurde ab 1702 durch einen größeren, französischen Garten ersetzt, den so genannte „holländische“ Kanäle durchzogen. Der Große Kanal bildet die Mittelachse. 1799/1823 wurde der Schlosspark nach Entwürfen Friedrich Ludwigs von Sckell zu einem Englischen Garten, einem Landschaftspark, umgestaltet. Die Grundstruktur des Barockgartens blieb aber erhalten. Der letzte wichtige Bau im Park war 1865 der Monopteros von Leo von Klenze, ein Rundtempel am Badenburger See.

Information

Schloss- und Gartenverwaltung Nymphenburg, Eingang 1, München, Tel. 089-179080, Fax 089-17908627; geöffnet April-15. Okt. 9–18 Uhr, Do 9–20 Uhr.
Im Marstallmuseum sind Staats- und Gala-Wagen und -Schlitten aus der einstigen „Hofwagenburg“, darunter sol-

For sunset try to be back at the palace building, then see the exciting colours of the garden and the front exterior, turn around and look into the fiery orb going down over the central water canal.
Not to forget, for families this area is a paradise. While the kids have space enough in the park to rollick about, to have much fun with the swans and many other water fowls, the adults can enjoy the magnificent buildings, at least from the outside.

Nymphenburg Castle

Prince Elector Ferdinand Maria gave Nymphenburg as a present to his wife Henriette Adelaide for the birthday of the heir to the throne.
So the construction started in 1664 with the central 5-storey building, the architectural style designed by Agostino Barelli, modelled on a typical suburban villa from northern Italy. To the west, the building faced a garden with water basins and founts.
From 1673 on, the interior of the building was designed by Enrico Zucalli.
In the 18th century, Nynphenburg Palace was to be completed as a Baroque complex by the heir of the throne, Prince Elector Max II Emanuel himself. The real work was pushed on not before the politically unsuccessful prince returned to Munich from exile in 1714. The palace has been enormously enlarged then by adding the orangery and the royal stable in the north and the south respectively, the building finally covering 1.5 km of length. The renown and experienced Joseph Effner took part of the planning and design.
1755–57 Prince Elector Max III Joseph commissioned a reconfiguration of the "Great Hall" in the central building. The famous artists Johann Baptist Zimmermann and François Cuvilliés the Elder created one of the major Rococo rooms in Germany. Lavishly decorated and with magnificent frescos, depicting the spring goddess "Flora" and her nymphs, whom the castle is named after.
From 1702 on the originally Italianate palace garden was transformed into a larger and French style garden crossed with numerous Dutch water canals.
Effner created the architectural highlight of the park, when he designed the four Baroque summer residences, arguably the most significant ones in whole Europe.
Finally between 1799 and 1823 the garden was transformed into an English style landscaped park by von Sckell without changing the basic structure of the Baroque garden.

Parkschloss Amalienburg

Parkschloss Badenburg

che Königs Ludwig II., gezeigt und zudem Reitausrüstungen aus der Sattelkammer der bayerischen Herrscher.
Das Museum „Nymphenburger Porzellan" präsentiert mit der Sammlung Bäuml die Geschichte der Porzellanmanufaktur von 1747, dem Jahr der Gründung durch Kurfürst Max III. Joseph, bis etwa 1920. Auch Arbeiten von Franz Anton Bustelli, dem bedeutendsten Porzellankünstler im 18. Jahrhundert, sind ausgestellt.
Die Museen haben die gleichen Öffnungszeiten wie das Schloss.

Verkehrsanbindung: S-Bahnlinien 12, 16, 17 und Buslinien 41, 65, 68 bis Romanplatz oder S-Bahnlinien 17 und Buslinie 41 bis Schloss Nymphenburg.

Parkschloss Amalienburg

„Das Rokoko hat kaum ein anderes Werk hervorgebracht, in dem seine besonderen Stileigenschaften, abgesehen von der hohen Qualität, so ausschließlich und so konzentriert zur Geltung käme.", schwärmte ein Kunsthistoriker im letzten Jahrhundert beim Anblick der Amalienburg.

Im Nymphenburger Schlosspark, südlich des großen Gartenparterres, ließ Kurfürst Karl Albrecht 1734 den Bau des Lust- und Jagdschlosses Amalienburg beginnen, das den Namen seiner Gattin Maria Amalia trägt, die es als Ausgangspunkt für ihre Fasanenjagden nutzte. Es war von François Cuvilliés d. Ä. geplant worden und wurde 1739 vollendet.
Das Lusthaus Amalienburg präsentiert sich als eingeschossiger Bau mit zentralem Kuppelraum, der zur Rückseite risalitartig ausspringt, während die Zugangsseite einen kleinen Ehrenhof aufweist.
Äußerst prächtig ist die Ausstattung des Schlosses, an welcher u. a. der Stuckateur Johann Baptist Zimmermann, der Holzbildhauer Joachim Dietrich und der Maler Joseph Pasqualin Moretti beteiligt waren. Die von Moretti geschaffenen Ornamentmalereien wurden teils erneuert. Erwähnenswert sind insbesondere die versilberten Dekorationen im Innern - Silber ist die Farbe des Mondes. Gelb und blau sind die Hintergrundgestaltungen der Räume. Hervorzuheben ist der runde, mit einer Flachkuppel versehene Spiegelsaal, dessen Deckenstuck Nymphen, Putten und Sinnbilder der Jagd zeigt und somit, wie die Statue der Jagdgöttin Diana auf den Zweck des Schlosses verweist.

Amalienburg Castle

Next to the Palace building on the south side is the "Amalienburg". Its ground plan balancing the elements of rectangle and circle, the elegantly curved front exterior, comparatively plain albeit with detailed ornaments, and the marvellous Rococo interior decoration are in perfect harmony with each other.
In the midst of the afternoon you might wander from the palace building throug the park allee, providing pleasant shade, and along a small water canal. After a mere 10 minutes walk you will reach "Amalienburg" castle, which is seated on a small open spot between the colourful summer trees.
Nothing really points out that it was originally intended as a hunting lodge. Overmore with your first step inside you dive into a Rococo decoration of flamboyant colours resplendent silver ornaments and rich stuccoes. Your outstanding experience will be the "Mirror Hall", where blue and silver as dominant colours, stucco works, carvings and mirrors are almost dispersing the room structure.
When you leave the building you might feel like awakening from a beautiful dream.

Information about history and architecture

1739 Prince Elector Karl Albrecht, who for three years, 1742–45, even ruled the Habsburg Empire, gave "Amalienburg" as a present to his wife Amalia. From here, she used to set off for pheasant-hunting. The hunting theme with related paintings and statues like that of hunting goddess Diana pervades most of the interior rooms.
The summer residence "Amalienburg" presents itself as a 1-tiered building of ionic formation and with a central dome.

Badenburg Castle

About 2 kilometres southwest from the Palace and adjacent to a lake of the same name, lies the summer residence "Badenburg". As the German name implies, it was a bathing pavilion, and in fact it housed the first heated indoor swimming bath in Europe.
setting off from "Amalienburg and heading for "Badenburg" you should make a leisure stroll of it. Signs will help you to find the way easily.
As a single or being with someone, you will enjoy the sounds, the colours, the unexpected romantic spots of the park.

Parkschloss Badenburg

Das „Badeschloss“ steht etwa 2 km westsüdwestlich von Schloss Nymphenburg entfernt und war als ein themenbezogenes Lusthaus, in diesem Falle zum Baden, gedacht. Impulse zum Bau soll Kurfürst Max Emanuel durch französische Bade-Appartements erhalten haben, doch hatte er sicher während seiner Kriegszüge in Ungarn in türkisch besetzten Gebieten türkische Badehäuser gesehen, die ihn zum Bau der Badenburg angeregt haben könnten.

Das Schloss setzt sich im Grundriss aus vier Einheiten zusammen, dem rechteckigen, an den Ecken abgerundeten Festsaal an der Nordseite, der ein Wasserparterre vorgelegt war, und dem in Bad, Spiel- und Schlafzimmer aufgegliederten Wohnbereich auf der Südseite, vor der sich ein Blumenparterre erstreckte. Beide Hauptseiten erschließen Freitreppen. Die Seiten des Schlosses waren wegen der Einbindung des Gebäudes in Baumreihen nicht als Schauseiten ausgebildet.

Im frühen 19. Jahrhundert erfolgte die Beseitigung des Stuckdekors der Fassaden, deren ursprüngliche Farbigkeit, ockerfarbige Gliederungen auf weißen Rücklagen, im Rahmen der Restaurierung 1983/84 neu gewonnen wurde.

Im Inneren sind die chinesischen Papiertapeten, die Vertäfelungen von Johann Adam Pichler und die Groteskenmalereien an der Decke des Schreibkabinetts von Nikolaus Gottfried Stuber sehenswert, ebenso wie die Stuckaturen im Festsaal.

Den Baderaum umgibt eine mit Stuckmarmor gestaltete Galerie. Das Becken war mit Bleiplatten ausgekleidet, darüber befanden sich holländische Fliesen. In technischer Hinsicht bemerkenswert ist der im Untergeschoss erhaltene Warmwasserkessel mit durchlaufender Rohrschlange.

Parkschloss Pagodenburg

Die Pagodenburg war das erste der im 18. Jahrhundert im Nymphenburger Park erbauten Lustschlösser (= franz.: maison de plaisance). Solche Lustschlösser konnten sehr verschiedene Dimensionen haben, die vom kleinen Pavillon bis hin zum Landschloss reichten. Sie dienten zumeist nur zum vorübergehenden Aufenthalt des Besitzers, insbesondere im Sommer. Die Gruppe der vier Lustschlösser in Nymphenburg gehört zu den bedeutendsten weltweit!

Die 1716-19 nach Entwürfen von Joseph Effner im nördlichen Teil des Parks errichtete Pagodenburg ist als zweigeschossiges Achteck mit vier kurzen Flügeln ausgebildet, so dass sich ein kreuzförmiger Grundriss ergibt. Hinter einer einst mit Vasen bekrönten Attika erhebt sich, nicht sichtbar, das flache Zeltdach. Die für die Barockzeit typischen „exo-

If you arrange to arrive at the lakeside opposite to the Badenburg castle somewhere between
4 and 5 p.m. summer time, you definitely have a breathtaking view at the "Amalienburg" reflected in the water and blooming in the late afternoon sunlight.

Sunlight falling at glancing incidence on a building facade will often grant you with rich colours in the shaded parts and clearly visible profiles in the sunlit parts at the same time.

Later you step into the bathing pavilion and within minutes, you feel amazed by the obvious side by side realisation of artistic furnishings and practical achievements especially in the bathing room down in the basement.

Information about history and architecture

Prince Elector Max Emanuel II commissioned Effner to build the "Badenburg" in the years 1718–21. He might have been stimulated for such a building by his experiences with Turkish bathing houses, which he gathered during his military campaign in Hungary.

The building's ground plan is made up of the rectangular festivity hall at the north side and the living area on the south side respectively, steps leading up to the entrances on both sides.

The interior is characterised by French Regency elements. There are Chinese wallpapers, paintings from Bertini, stucco works from Dubut and frescoes from Amigoni.

The bathing room is decked with blue and white Dutch tiles. Its ceiling is adorned with frescoes depicting mythological bathing scenes.

Pagodenburg Castle

Not far distant from the "Badenburg" in the northern part of the park, romantically seated on a small lake is the "Pagodenburg", the first of the 4 Nymphenburg summer residences built in the Baroque century. As the name implies it offers some exotic art impressions.

Looking from close at the two-tiered building you might be impressed by the rococo style front exterior. Stepping inside, you find the ground floor furnished in European style with Dutch tiles and ornament paintings in white – blue. The upper floor surprises with rich coloured chinoiseries, pagoda motifs, wallpapers made from silk or from rice-straw and some paintings in old Japanese style.

If you need some rest now, you will enjoy sitting on one of the wooden benches in front of the building or right on the water's edge.

Parkschloss Pagodenburg

tischen“ Motive finden sich in der Ausstattung in Form von „asiatischen“ und „indianischen“ Elementen und importierten chinesischen Lackarbeiten. Auch der Name des Schlosses verweist auf den asiatischen Kontinent.
Schon 1767 kam es zu Änderungen am Außenbau, als die Stuckaturen nach Entwürfen von François Cuvilliés d. Ä. im Rahmen einer Renovierung in Stilformen des Rokoko abgeändert wurden. Die Farbfassung der Rokoko-Zeit, helle Beige- und Grautöne, wurde 1985-87 rekonstruiert.
Die Innenräume wurden mit holländischen Fliesen zwischen Stuckaturen, Täfelungen und mit dekorativen Malereien ausgestaltet.

Parkschloss Magdalenenklause

Als drittes der vier Nymphenburger Parkschlösser entstand 1725-28 die Magdalenenklause. Sie gehört zu den frühen „Kunstruinen“ in Deutschland: Im 18. Jahrhundert wurden künstlich errichtete Ruinen ebenso wie künstliche Grotten und Einsiedeleien (so genannte Klausen) zunehmend wichtige Elemente barocker Gärten und Parks, insbesondere in Frankreich, England und Deutschland.
Ruinen, echte und künstliche, waren seit der Zeit des späten Rokoko, begründet durch die ästhetische Literatur, Symbole für Abschied und Tod. In Parks sollten sie eine sentimentale Stimmung verbreiten und Bezüge zum Mittelalter und der Antike herstellen.
Die Magdalenenklause, die als Einsiedelei (= franz. eremitage) im „einsamen“, aber doch dem Hauptschloss Nymphenburg nahe gelegenen Teil der Parkanlage errichtet wurde, ist eine fantasievolle Mischung aus gotischen, maurischen und antiken Formen: Während an der Kapelle gotische Motive aufgegriffen wurden, folgt die Gestaltung des Giebels am Eingang Vorbildern italienischer Ruinen.
Dabei handelt es sich aber nicht nur um Kulissenarchitektur, die Klause war auch bewohnbar. Im Innern bestimmen barocke Gestaltungsprinzipien die beinahe symmetrische Raumaufteilung. Es finden sich dort getäfelte Wohnräume und die zweiteilige Kapelle, die mit Muscheln, ursprünglich gefärbten Kieseln und Stuckskulpturen reich ausgestaltet ist und den Charakter einer Park-Grotte hat.

Information

(gilt für Amalienburg, Badenburg, Magdalenenklause und Pagodenburg im Nymphenburger Park)
Schloss- und Gartenverwaltung Nymphenburg, Schloss Nymphenburg, Eingang 1, München, Tel. 089-179080, Fax 089-17908627. April-15. Okt. 9-18 Uhr, Do 9-20 Uhr.
Verkehrsanbindung: S-Bahnlinie 17 und Buslinie 41 bis Schloss Nymphenburg.

Information about history and architecture:

From 1716 to 1719 the "Pagodenburg" had been constructed, designed by Joseph Effner as a 2 - storey octagonal building with 4 short wings, resulting in a cross shaped ground plan. Not later than 1767 the front exterior was renovated and changed to Rococo style mainly based on stucco works designed by François Cuvilliés the Elder. Inside Anton Gumpp created many of the decorative paintings on either floor.

Magdalenenklause Castle

A few steps northwest from the palace building hidden in a forest part of the park is the "Magdalenenklause". It was built as an artificial ruin, a very popular kind of building in Baroque gardens, and intended as a hermitage - a retreat for contemplation and prayers. Late morning to noon time the sunlight is bright enough to light up the building which all of a sudden emerges from the gloom of the forest.
What a contrast to the Baroque and Rococo appearance of the other three summer residences! Here you are confronted with a ruin-like exterior made from brick stones mainly, which had but one purpose: to create a sentimental feeling at the visitor and to prepare him for the themes of ancient times.
Inside the hermitage the ruin-impression is maintained by the two-part chapel, the walls and ceiling of which are covered with mussel shells, colourful pebbles and stuccoes of mythical creatures. There are also living rooms albeit with simple furnishings, plain panels and a few religious paintings.
Finally you might not feel unhappy to leave that strange building and to rush through the adjacent wood back into the open and sunny area of the park.

Information about history und architecture

1725–28 the hermitage "Magdalenenklause" was built basing on the design from Joseph Effner. For the European Baroque gardens and parks artificial as well as real ruins became elements of growing significance. Ruins in the aesthetic literature of the late Rococo period symbolised farewell and death.
The antique, gothic and even Moorish architectural elements of the "Magdalenenklause" are put together in a highly imaginative building.

Schloss Schleißheim

mit Neuem Schloss, Schloss Lustheim und Altem Schloss

Vor Ort

Wenn Sie (Hobby-)Fotograf sind, empfehlen wir Ihnen, nicht später als 7.00 Uhr morgens nach Oberschleißheim zu kommen. Der Schlosspark, der das Neue und das Alte Schloss Schleißheim sowie Schloss Lustheim beherbergt, öffnet bereits um 7.30 Uhr, wenn die Innenräume, je nach Jahreszeit, auch erst später zu besichtigen sind. Als Belohnung für das frühe Aufstehen erwartet Sie das Licht der aufgehenden Sonne, wie es schöner nicht sein könnte. Am besten stellen Sie sich in die Nähe einer der großen Statuen und genießen den Blick auf das Schloss mit seiner barocken Fassade.
Lassen Sie Ihren Blick auch über die barocken Parkanlage mit ihren unzähligen geometrisch angelegten Blumenbeeten und Wegen schweifen.

Informationen zur Geschichte und Architektur

Zu den bedeutendsten Schlössern der Barockzeit in Deutschland gehört die Gruppe der drei Schlösser bei Oberschleißheim, etwa 20 km von München entfernt. Den Bau eines ersten Schlosses ließ Herzog Wilhelm V. beginnen, der 1597 die Schwaige Schleißheim, in einsamer Moorgegend gelegen, erworben hatte. Ab 1598 entstanden ein Gutshof und das Herrenhaus als Villa suburbana (= vorstädtische, landwirtschaftlich ausgerichtete Villa) und „fürstliche Eremitage“, umgeben von Klausen und Waldkapellen.
Dem Sohn Wilhelms, Herzog Maximilian, genügte das Haus seines Vaters nicht mehr. So begann er 1616/17, das spätere so genannte Alte Schloss zu erbauen. Spätestens ab 1683 plante Kurfürst Maximilian II. das parallel dazu erbaute Neue Schloss. Insofern blieb das Alte Schloss mit seiner Ausstattung lange Zeit weitgehend erhalten. Erst im Zweiten Weltkrieg wurde es 1944 größtenteils zerstört.

Neues Schloss Schleißheim

„Dieses ist ein prächtiger, eines Fürsten, ja eines Königs oder Kaisers würdiger Palast, dessen Schönheit, Ordnung und Regularität der Baukunst von außen einem gleich in die Augen fällt und zu dessen großen Schönheiten, die man von innen mit Erstaunen erblickt, gleichsam eine vergnügliche Vorbereitung macht“, so schwärmte Matthias Diesel um 1720.
Die von Kurfürst Max Emanuel um 1700 begonnene barocke Schlossanlage mit einer Gesamtlänge von 330 Me-

Your Sightseeing

Just 20 km north of Munich there is located the suburb Schleißheim, famous for its group of three castles: the New and the Old Palace of Schleißheim and the Hunting and Garden Lodge Lustheim. Together with the Palace Garden, they constitute one of the major Baroque complexes in Europe.
Here you have the occasion for an unforgettable sightseeing event. However you should invest nothing less than a complete day (a weekday, because on weekend the palace area might be heavily crowded) at best weather conditions and with blue sky. Then you find the proper scenery for a baroque performance.
The combination of and the alternation between wandering through the park and exploring the buildings are a guarantee of a unique experience.

Information about history and architecture

1597 Duke Wilhelm V acquired the manor house "Schleißheim", after his abdication he decided to live here in solitude and religious contemplation.
1617–23 Duke and Prince Elector Maximilian I had built the "Old Castle", a masterpiece of late Renaissance.
1684–88 Prince Elector Max Emanuel II commissioned to build the "Lustheim Castle" as a hunting and garden lodge.
1701–1726 Prince Elector Max Emanuel II had built the "New Castle". In case that he would have been elected as Emperor, this castle was intended to become the new residence.
In 1715 after his return from exile in France, the Prince Elector Max Emanuel commissioned the French garden architect Dominique Girard to complete the Baroque Park.

New Castle Schleißheim

The "New Castle" - the real "Schleißheim palace" - spreads out, facing the "Old Castle" in the west and "Lustheim castle" in the east,
Prince Elector Max Emanuel II had built it as the embodiment of his imperial dreams, which eventually never came true. However, relating to this motivation, plans and designs as to dimensions and magnificence had to be modelled on the palaces of Versailles and Vienna.

Neues Schloss Schleißheim

Neues Schloss Schleißheim

tern gehört zu den bedeutendsten Residenzen aus der Zeit des Absolutismus. Die Ausstattung der letzteren um 1720 gehört zu den besten ihrer Art in ganz Europa. Immer wieder kam es zu Unterbrechungen beim Schlossbau. Als Max Emanuel 1726 starb, war es unvollendet und nicht komplett eingerichtet.
Bis ins 19. Jahrhundert wurde am Neuen Schloss gebaut, die barocken Pläne wurden aber nie ganz verwirklicht.
1975 eröffneten hier die Bayerischen Staatsgemäldesammlungen München die Staatsgalerie europäischer Malerei des Barock, die zu den eindrucksvollsten Sammlungen ihrer Art in Deutschland zählt.

Schloss Lustheim

Anstelle der Renatusklause, einem Parkbau, ließ Kurfürst Max II. Emanuel nur 600 Meter entfernt vom Alten Schloss anlässlich seiner Heirat mit der kaiserlichen Tochter Maria Antonia ab 1684 das Schloss Lustheim als Jagd- und Lustschloss in der Art eines italienischen Gartencasinos errichten.
Hinter dem zweigeschossigen Schloss mit Belvedere sollten in einem Halbkreis Galerien, Bauten für Hofkavaliere und Bedienstete sowie Orangerien entstehen. Schleißheim war in das mehrere der kurfürstlichen Schlösser verbindende Kanalsystem einbezogen, und mit der Anlage eines ringförmig geführten Kanals wurde Schloss Lustheim letztlich zu einem Wasserschloss auf einer runden Insel.
Umgeben war das Schloss von Blumenbeeten und Fontänen. Im Innern gab es acht kleine, „sehr wohl angelegte Fürstenzimmer“ und in der Mitte einen großen Saal. Diesen zweigeschossigen Saal flankieren die beiden Appartements des Kurfürsten und seiner Gemahlin.
Seit 1971 beherbergt Schloss Lustheim als Zweigmuseum des Bayerischen Nationalmuseums die „Meißener Porzellan-Sammlung Stiftung Ernst Schneider“, die im Erd- und im Untergeschoss präsentiert wird. Zur Sammlung, die den Zeitraum von den ersten Experimenten des Alchimisten und Erfinders des europäischen Hartporzellans, Johann Friedrich Böttger (1682–1719), bis zur Meißener Porzellanproduktion aus der Zeit des 7-jährigen Krieges (1756–63) umfasst, gehören u. a. Geschirr, Tafelaufsätze und (Tier-)Figuren.

Information

Neues Schloss/Hofgarten Schleißheim & Schloss Lustheim, Max-Emanuel-Platz 1, Schleißheim; Info: Schloss- und Gartenverwaltung Schleißheim-Dachau, Max-Emanuel-Platz 1, Oberschleißheim, Tel. 089-315872-0, Fax 089-315872-50.
Zugänglichkeit für Gehbehinderte: Eingangshalle und Parterre des Neuen Schlosses sind über eine Rampe zu erreichen. Mit einem Lift gelangt man ins 1. OG.
Verkehrsanbindung: S-Bahnlinie 1 bis Oberschleißheim.

The elegant French baroque style dominates the facades and the sumptuous interior decoration as well.
The Great Hall, the Victorian Hall and the Great Gallery are the most significant rooms of the building.

Information about history and architecture

Commissioned by Prince Elector Max Emanuel II in the late 1680s, the building of the "New Castle" was started in 1701-1704, the plans have been designed by Enrico Zuccalli. The construction was done under Joseph Effner and, following an interruption of several years caused by the Prince's exile, has been completed from 1719-26.
The Palace, made up of a central building, connecting wings and corner pavilions on either side, came out with a total length of 330 meters.
Well renowned artists as Johann Baptist Zimmermann and Cosmas Damian Asam took part in the creation of the furnishings.
Zuccalli also started the layout of the Baroque Park, Dominique Girard completed the work until 1726.
The Schleißheim Palace Park is one of the few castle parks in Germany having retained its Baroque layout and character unchanged.

Lustheim Castle

Embedded into the Baroque Park of "Schleißheim Palace" lies the "Lustheim Castle", an extravagant Italianate building. It is facing a delightful flower garden in the west and a more open landscaped garden in the east. A circular water canal, spanned with small wrought-iron bridges, surrounds the whole complex.

Your Sightseeing

Standing at the big fountain bordering the "New Castle's" garden to the east, you turn around and have that spectacular view eastward along the central water canal at the Lustheim castle. With the morning sun in your eyes, maybe some haze still over the water, you get an impression like that on a romantic painting.
It is the geometrical strength of the Baroque layout and the stillness of nature, which generate inside you that sentiment of clearness and emotional balance.
Arriving at the castle in the midst of the morning, the eastern side is the attractive one. The sunlit facade of the building and the spaceous garden with the old large trees invite you to stay.
However, you might soon feel impatient to see the treasures inside the castle. It houses an excellent collection of porcelain, comprising pieces from the early period of Johann Friedrich Böttger, figurines from Kandler and numerous pieces of tableware out of the "Meißen" production dated from the 7-years-war-period.
After having enjoyed the delicate beauty of the porcelain art, you emerge into the natural atmosphere outside.

Schloss Lustheim

Neues Schloss
Schleißheim

Altes Schloss Schleißheim

Im Gegensatz zu den Schlössern und Residenzen sind die Stadtpalais nur von außen zu besichtigen. Die Innenräume sind Besuchern nicht zugänglich, da sie städtischen Einrichtungen offiziell genutzt werden.
Dennoch sollten Sie sie bei Ihrem Gang durch die Stadt nicht übersehen, prägen ihre Lage, Architektur und Gestaltung doch nicht unwesentlich das Gesicht der Stadt München.

Altes Schloss Schleißheim

Das Äußere des zweigeschossigen Schlosses wurde verhältnismäßig schlicht gehalten. Eine zweiläufige überdachte Treppe, unter der eine künstliche Grotte angelegt war, führte zum Eingang des großen Saales. Dieser Saal mit Tonnengewölbe besaß Rahmenstuck mit Medaillons, die, passend zum Charakter des Schlosses, das Landleben priesen.
Wie auch in Nymphenburg, ja mehr noch als dort, prägen Kanäle das Erscheinungsbild, indem sie das Ensemble der drei Schlösser in Längen von 350 und 1500 m umfassen: alle Schlösser stehen somit auf einer großen, untergliederten Insel.
Nach dem Zweiten Weltkrieg wurde das Alte Schloss wieder aufgebaut, um die Sammlung Gertrud Weinhold („Das Gottesjahr und seine Feste“ als Teilmuseum des Bayerischen Nationalmuseums) und eine Sammlung zur Landeskunde Ost- und Westpreußens „Es war ein Land ...“ aufzunehmen.

Information

Schloss- und Gartenverwaltung Schleißheim-Dachau, Max-Emanuel-Platz 1, Oberschleißheim, Tel. 089-315872-0, Fax 089-315872-50; geöffnet Di-So 10-17 Uhr; Sonderführungen auf Anfrage.
Verkehrsanbindung: S-Bahnlinie 1 bis Oberschleißheim.

Through the colossal pillars in the foreground and over the flowered garden, your view is caught on the straight line of the canal with the Schleißheim Palace about 2 km distant in the background.

Information about history and architecture

In place of an older park building, the "Renatus" hermitage, Prince Elector Max Emanuel II in 1684 had built "Lustheim castle", intended as a hunting lodge and summer residence. The design from Enrico Zucalli was modelled on an Italianate garden casino, the facades were copies of the "Villa Madama" in Rome. The central building, dominated on its front exterior by twin pillars, is set between two lower side tracts.
The banqueting hall and the private rooms of the Prince are adorned with ceiling frescoes glorifying the hunting goddess Diana. 1686–87 Johann Anton Gumpp, Giovanni Trubillion and Francesco Rosa created these ceiling paintings, arguably the first in a secular Bavarian building.

Old Castle Schleißheim

Your Sightseeing

Coming from the "Lustheim Castle" and heading back for the Palace, make a stroll of it. Leave the path along the central canal and explore the aside parts of the park. They too are geometrically arranged and within a moment, you feel like in a labyrinth.
After a 15-minutes-walk, you emerge in the Palace garden, where you cannot withstand to linger in for a while. Now the facade of the palace is shaded and it appears in rich colours.
After having visited the Palace interior (see above), you would like to approach the "Old Castle". Now in the midst of the afternoon, the sun lights up the main front, facing to the west. The building and garden appear to harmonise, albeit their quite plain outer architecture.
From close, it reveals a charming character. Inside you might marvel at the "Great Hall" with its impressive barrel vaulting. Moreover, there is a special department of the "Bavarian National Museum", exhibiting a considerable collection of religious art pieces.

Information about history and architecture

From 1598 on, Duke Wilhelm V had acquired a countryside estate, located in secluded moorland and built a manor house as a "Villa Suburbana". He decided to live there after his abdication in solitude and contemplation.
His son Maximilian, later as Prince Elector Maximilian I commissioned to build the "Old Castle" on the site of the manor house, according to the design from the ducal master mason Heinrich Schön the Elder.
The two-sided staircase leads to the entrance of the "Great Hall" decorated with stuccoes from Peter Candid.

Palais der Grafen Preysing

Das Preysing-Palais, nicht zu verwechseln mit dem Palais (Neuhaus-)Preysing in der Prannerstraße, steht hinter der Feldherrnhalle, zwischen Residenz- und Theatinerstraße, auf einem wegen der Straßengabelung unregelmäßigen Grundstück. Die Straßen teilten sich hier, vom (nicht erhaltenen) Schwabinger Tor der Stadtbefestigung herkommend. Der Bauplatz des Palastes liegt zwischen der Residenz und der Theatiner-Kirche und somit zwischen zwei stadtbildprägenden Baukomplexen.

Vor Ort

Das optische Highlight dieses Gebäudes ist die Fassade, die sich zur Residenz hin erstreckt. Im frühen Morgenlicht wirken das Farbenspiel und die Stuckaturen besonders eindrucksvoll. Durch das Palais führt eine elegante Einkaufspassage. Versäumen Sie nicht, einen Blick auf die eindrucksvolle Treppe und die reichen Wandmalereien im Inneren zu werfen.

Informationen zur Geschichte und Architektur

Als „erstes Rokoko-Palais in München" wurde das 1723/29 für Johann Maximilian IV. Graf von Preysing-Hohenaschau nach Plänen von Joseph Effner errichtete Bauwerk bezeichnet. Die drei Fassaden des Palastes sind verschieden aufwändig gestaltet. Die Hauptfassade erstreckt sich nach Osten, zur Residenz hin. Die Fassaden des dreigeschossigen, verputzten Baues mit Mezzanin strukturiert ein flacher Mittelrisalit mit Portal und Giebel. Effner entwarf einen Palastbau, der sich hinsichtlich baulicher Details und der Dekoration an französischen und österreichischen Architekten orientierte, aber durchaus auch Individualität und Eigenständigkeit erkennen lässt. Neu und vorbildgebend für München war die Verwendung innenarchitektonischer Dekorationselemente (Stuck) für den Außenbau.
Bei der Kriegszerstörung des Gebäudes 1944 gingen die drei bis dahin noch erhaltenen historischen Raumausstattungen verloren. Zudem wurde das Treppenhaus, das im oberen Teil mit einer zweiläufigen Treppe ausgestattet war, erheblich beschädigt. 1946 kam es zum Abbruch der West- und Teilen der Südfassade, die 1958/60 weitgehend rekonstruiert wurden. Dabei konnten Teile des originalen Stucks von Johann Baptist Zimmermann übernommen werden. Die Anzahl der Etagen sowie die Anordnung der Innenräume ist neu, der einstige Innenhof wurde überbaut.

Information

Residenzstr. 27, München.
Verkehrsanbindung: U-Bahnlinien 3/4/5/6 bis Odeonsplatz.

Different to the Royal Palaces, the Town Palaces do not offer a complete sightseeing event. Their interior is not open to public, because they are in official use still, there are no gardens or parks to stroll in. However, their location, architecture and especially their façades play a significant role for the visitor's optical impression from the city.
This holds for Munich just as much as for Vienna, Paris and other historical capitals. To get this impression does not really depend, on which weekday you visit them. You see them on a working day or Saturday, this will give you a vivid impression, how important those buildings are as a background for city life, similar to a stage set in the theatre.
If you are more deeply interested in their architecture, a visit on Sunday is preferable.
The high-ranking noble families of the country had to have a Town Palace for their own representation at the royal court as well as in the city's life.
The "Town Palace of the Counts Preysing", easily the most important one, is closely located between the "Royal Residence" and the "Theatiner Church" – two landmarks of Munich. Its main front faces the Residence to the east, and it is bordering the "Feldherrnhalle" (the "Commanders Hall") to the north.

Your Sightseeing

The optical highlight of this palace is the exterior of its main front.
The early morning light before 9 a.m. makes the façade most appealing, because it lights up the comparative dark colours and at the same time reveals the rich structure of the Regency stuccoes.
There is a passageway through the Palace, where you might enjoy an elegant shopping mall, and look at the flamboyant triple staircase adorned with wall decorations.

Information about history and architecture

The "Town Palace of the Counts Preysing" constitutes the earliest Rococo Palace in Munich. It was built by Joseph Effner between 1723–29 for Johann Maximilian IV Count from Preysing-Hohenaschenau.
As an architectural novelty, the facade was decorated with stuccoes, up to then only applied to the interior of buildings. Later buildings of Munich have been modelled on this.

Palais Törring

Wie mehrere öffentliche Bauten in München ging auch die Hauptpost aus einem Adelssitz hervor: 1747-54 entstand das Adelspalais Törring(-Jettenbach), eine Vierflügelanlage, für die gräfliche Familie von Törring nach Entwürfen von Ignaz Anton Gunetzrhainer unter Beteiligung François Cuvilliés'.

Vor Ort

Verbinden Sie Ihren Besuch des Palais mit einer Pause im dortigen Bistro. Zu jeder Tageszeit bietet sich von der Loggia aus ein reizvoller Blick über den gesamten Max-Joseph-Platz.

Informationen zur Geschichte und Architektur

In den Jahren 1835/38 erfolgte der Umbau des Rokoko-Palastes zur Hauptpost, wozu der Architekt Leo von Klenze die Planungen übernahm. Eine damals erfolgte seitliche Erweiterung des Baus war nicht unumstritten. Heute hingegen gilt die an der italienischen Renaissance-Architektur orientierte Architektur der Loggia als eine gelungene städtebauliche Lösung.
Die Westfassade sowie das Vestibül und das Treppenhaus wurden bei der Bombardierung der Stadt 1944 zerstört. In den Neubau von 1949/56 hat man dann die Bogenhalle integriert, und in die Schalterhalle ein Barock-Portal eingefügt.
Bemerkenswert ist eine Gruppe von neun überlebensgroßen, grau gefassten allegorischen Figuren aus Holz, die Johann Baptist Straub für das Vestibül des Palastes fertigte. Zwei wurden in der Vorhalle der Hauptpost aufgestellt, die übrigen sieben ins Bayerische Nationalmuseum verbracht.

Information

Residenzstr. 2, München. Die Schalterhalle ist frei zugänglich.
Verkehrsanbindung: U-Bahnlinien 3/4/5/6 bis Odeonsplatz.

Bordering the stately Max-Joseph-Platz to the south, is the "Törring Palace". With its Italianate Renaissance loggia it brings out the light feature, the balance to the massive front exteriors of the two other major buildings flanking this place: the Royal Residence and the "National Theatre".

Your Sightseeing

It is the wee hours of the morning, when you should approach this sight: The sunlight now illuminates the colourful paintings on the red interior wall of the arcade loggia. Inside the loggia, there is a bistro, where you might have an early breakfast. From your seat, you will appreciate the spectacular view through the loggia's slender pillars over the entire Josephplatz.
Take it as a very attractive option, to visit this same spot at the dusk or evening hours on a warm summer day.

Information about history and architecture

1747-54 the Noble Palace for the Count's family was built as a 4-wing complex, based on the design from Ignaz Anton Gunetzrhainer.
In the years 1835 to 38 the Rococo style palace has been reconfigured according to the plans from Leo von Klenze, and henceforth used as the Main Post Office of Munich. The old Baroque portal is still today incorporated into the post hall.
Klenze has modelled the arcade loggia on the Foundling House in Florence designed by Brunelleschi.
Johann Baptist Straub has created nine larger-than-life allegorical figures, two of them still positioned in the entrance hall, and the rest are exhibited in the Bavarian National Museum.

Palais Törring

Palais Leuchtenberg

Der Vorgängerbau des Bayerischen Finanzministeriums entstand 1816/21 als Stadtpalais Leuchtenberg, als erstes der „Monumentalgebäude“ vor dem 1816 abgebrochenen Schwabinger Tor der Münchner Stadtbefestigung. Bauherr war Herzog Eugen v. Leuchtenberg (Eugène Beauharnais), ein Schwiegersohn König Maximilians I. Joseph, für den Leo von Klenze die Baupläne lieferte. Der Herzog, der an der Stabilität der wirtschaftlichen Verhältnisse zweifelte, hatte von Klenze den Auftrag erteilt, den Bau so zu gestalten, dass er gegebenenfalls kurzfristig in ein Hotel umgestaltet werden könnte.

Vor Ort

Vom Reiterstandbild Königs Ludwig I. haben Sie den besten Blick auf das Gebäude und den gesamten Odeonsplatz mit der Theatinerkirche, der Residenz und der Feldherrnhalle. Von hier aus sind es nur wenige Schritte bis zum Wittelsbacher Platz, wo schon das nächste Palais, das Palais Ludwig-Ferdinand, auf Sie wartet.

Informationen zur Geschichte und Architektur

In den 1870er Jahren wurde der Palast dann infolge eines Besitzerwechsels „Palais Prinz Luitpold“ genannt.
Als erster Bau im Bereich der Ludwigstraße beeinflusste das Palais die spätere Bebauung des Odeonsplatzes und die Außengestaltung des Odeons selbst, das 1826-28 ebenfalls nach dem Entwurf von Leo von Klenze errichtet wurde! Das Palais Leuchtenberg ist ein schlichter klassizistischer Bau mit einer klaren Außengliederung und wenig reliefierten Fassaden. Es gilt als der erste klassizistische Bau in Mitteleuropa, orientiert an den italienischen Vorbildern der Neo-Renaissance, und wirkte stilprägend für das südliche Teilstück der Ludwigstraße.
Noch im 19. Jahrhundert wurde schon Kritik am Palast geübt. So heißt es 1876 im „Bautechnischen Führer durch München“, bezogen auf die Bauvorgaben des Herzogs für die Innengestaltung: „Es ist demnach die Anordnung einfach und ohne wesentliches Interesse, die Treppenhausbildung sogar unerfreulich kahl.“
Wir können das heute leider nicht mehr nachvollziehen, brannte der Palast doch infolge von Luftangriffen im Zweiten Weltkrieg 1943 und 1945 aus, erhalten blieben nur die Fassaden. Diese fielen dann 1962 einem Totalabbruch zum Opfer, auf den1963–66 der Neubau eines Stahlbetonskelettbaues folgte, dem eine das Erscheinungsbild des Palais rekonstruierende Backsteinfassade mit einer Steingussgliederung vorgeblendet wurde. Lediglich das Südportal ist größtenteils noch original.

Information

Odeonsplatz 4, München
Verkehrsanbindung: U-Bahnlinien 3/4/5/6 bis Odeonsplatz.

The "Leuchtenberg Palace" located at the "Odeonsplatz", is the largest of the Noble Town Palaces in Munich. It was built for Duke Eugen v. Leuchtenberg (the former Eugène Beauharnais, stepson of Napoleon), son-in-law of Bavarian King Max I Joseph. Later, Prince Regent Luitpold of Bavaria resided in this Palace, and today it houses the Bavarian State Department for Finances.

Your Sightseeing

Again it is the very early morning light, which brings out the clearness of the classical facade and the building's solid architecture. Your best viewing position is right in front of the equestrian statue showing King Ludwig I From here, you cannot only overlook the "Leuchtenberg Palace", but turning around you will appreciate the panorama view over the entire Odeonsplatz with its landmarks "Theatiner Church", "Royal Residence" and "Commanders Hall".
The main entrance side of the Palace, facing to the southwest is most impressive in the late afternoon sunlight. Looking at this façade in front of you and to the east front of the "Ludwig-Ferdinand Palace", you find yourself on a short through road from the Odeonsplatz to the Wittelsbach-Platz. For just a moment, you might feel like in the "Ideal Town" of the Urbino Renaissance painting.

Information about history and architecture

The "Leuchtenberg Palace" was built 1816–21 according to the plans from Leo von Klenze. It is regarded as the first example of "Neo Renaissance" Architecture in Europe. Klenze has modelled his design on the famous "Palazzo Farnese" in Rome.

Palais Leuchtenberg

Palais im ehemaligen Adelsviertel

mit dem Erzbischöflichen Palais, Palais Gise, Palais Preysing und Palais Portia

Der Wittelsbacher Platz, in unmittelbarer Nähe zum Odeonsplatz gelegen, ist sicher einer der attraktivsten Plätze Münchens. Er wird von drei überaus sehenswerten Gebäuden eingerahmt: dem Arco-Palais, dem Palais Ludwig Ferdinand und der rückwärtigen Front des Odeons. Außerdem befinden sich in unmittelbarer Nähe das Erzbischöfliche Palais, das Palais Gise sowie das Palais Portia.

Vor Ort

Unübersehbar und majestätisch präsentiert sich Ihnen das bronzene Reiterstandbild des Kurfürsten Maximilian I., wenn Sie sich dem Wittelsbacher Platz nähern. Dann öffnet sich der Platz und bietet architektonisch ein beeindruckendes harmonisches Gesamtbild.
Alle genannten Palais sind nur von außen zu besichtigen.
Wer sich an den prachtvollen Fassaden satt gesehen hat, dem sei ein Bummel durch die Brienner Straße mit ihren exklusiven Geschäften und einladenden Cafés empfohlen.

Erzbischöfliches Palais

Als „Münchens schönstes Rokoko-Palais“ gilt das von François Cuvilliés d. Ä. entworfene, 1733–37 erbaute Palais Holnstein. Kurfürst Karl Albrecht (1726–42) ließ den prächtigen Bau anstelle dreier Bürgerhäuser für seinen illegitimen Sohn Franz Ludwig Graf von Holnstein (1723–80) errichten. 72 Jahre lang bewohnte später die gräfliche Familie von Königsfeld den Palast, bevor dann 1821 der Erzbischof der kurz zuvor neu begründeten Diözese München-Freising hier seinen Sitz nahm. Und noch heute residiert hier der jeweilige Erzbischof. Im Laufe der Zeit fanden entsprechend verschiedene Namen für den Palast Verwendung, so „Palast des Grafen Holnstein“, „Graf-Königsfeld-Palast“, „Erzbischöfliches Palais“ und „Erzbischofshof“.

Information

Kardinal-Faulhaber-Str. 7, München

Coming from the elegant shopping avenue Brienner Street, just opposite to the Wittelsbacher Platz turn into Amiraplatz. Heading south, you emerge into the Kardinal-Faulhaber Straße which together with its side street Pranner Straße constitutes the former noble district of Munich, dotted with magnificent Baroque Town Palaces.

Your Sightseeing

Being there in the mid to the late afternoon, you will be rewarded with one of the most attractive views in Munich: as you step south, the mighty brick towers of the gothic Cathedral - the number one landmark of Munich - come into position right between the facades of the Baroque Palaces.
At first on the left side of the street, does the "Archiepiscopal Palace" impress you with its massive front exterior. Then, to the right you turn into the Pranner Straße and the view that meets you here is dominated by several beautiful buildings, the "Palace Neuhaus-Preysing" and the "Gise Palace" amongst them. Both reveal extravagant Rococo façades with rich ornaments and superb colours.
Turning back into the Kardinal-Faulhaber Straße and heading for the south, on the left side you are confronted with the Portia Palace, the Italianate architecture and the baroque façade of which merge into a harmonious whole.

The Arc Bishop’s Palace

(Erzbischöfliches Palais): The "Palace Holnstein" is arguably the most brilliant Rococo Palace of Munich. Today its official name is the "Archbishop´s Palace", because the archbishops of Munich-Freising since 1818 are residing here. On catholic holidays, the building is decorated with flowers, trees and flags.
In 1737, Prince Elector Karl Albrecht had built the magnificent Palace as a residence for his illegitimate son Count Franz Ludwig von Holstein.
The 3-tiered building has a first Mezzanine floor and above it the two main storeys, which are structured by colossal pilasters. The three middle axes of the facade are brought out with a portal, a balcony and a gable. Its stucco works have been made by Johann Baptist Zimmermann.

straße
dinal-Faulhaber-Str.

Erzbischöfliches Palais

Palais Gise

Das Palais wurde um 1765 wahrscheinlich von dem Hofbaumeister "Lespillez" für die Familie der Grafen "Arco-Taufkirchen" erbaut. Es entstand ein ansehnlichesGebäude des späten Rokoko, architektonisch und kusthistorisch bereits auf der Schwelle zum Klassizismus.Die Fassade mit ihren Strukturen wirkt eher dekorativ als funktional.

Information

Prannerstr. 9, München

Gise Palace

The "Gise Palace" was constructed around 1765, probably by the court architect "Lespilliez".for the family of counts "Arco-Taufkirchen.

It shows off as a resplendent late Rococo building, however in terms of architecture and art history already on the threshold of the classicism era. The façade of the building appears decorative rather than functional.

(Neuhaus)Preysing Palace

Palais Gise

Palais (Neuhaus)Preysing

Palais Portia

Palais (Neuhaus)Preysing

Der heutige Name „Palais Preysing“ geht auf die letzte adelige Besitzerfamilie des Palastes zurück, die bis 1923 hier ansässig war. Häufig kommt es zu Verwechslungen mit dem Preysing-Palais an der Rückseite der Feldherrnhalle zwischen Residenz- und Theatinerstraße.
Weder die genaue Bauzeit, noch der Architekt des Palais (Neuhaus-)Preysing konnten bisher ermittelt werden, doch wurde der Bau möglicherweise um 1735/40 unter Johann Franz Maria Freiherr von Neuhaus (1687–1752) begonnen. Wegen der Fassadengestaltung wurde der Entwurf des Palastes wiederholt François Cuvilliés d.Ä. zugeschrieben, was jedoch inzwischen wider bezweifelt wird.

Information

Prannerstr. 2, München

Palais Portia

Das Palais im Kreuzviertel unweit der Residenz entstand 1693/94 durch den Umbau eines Wohnhauses des kurfürstlichen Truchsessen Hanns Sigmund Graf Ahaim zum Stadtpalais für Maria Anna Katharina Gräfin Fugger und ihren Mann, den Oberhofmeister und Vorsitzenden des Geh. Rates, Paul Reichsgraf Fugger zu Kirchberg und Weißenhorn. Das „große Fuggerische Haus“, wie es genannt wurde, gehörte zu den ersten großen privaten Adelspalais in München.
Als Geschenk Kurfürst Albrechts kam das Gebäude später in den Besitz der Gräfin Portia.

Information

Kardinal-Faulhaber-Str. 12, München
Verkehrsanbindung (gilt für alle o. g. Palais):
S-Bahnlinien 1-8 bis Marienplatz oder U-Bahnlinien 3/4/5/6 bis Odeonsplatz.

According to designs from Cuvilliés, the Palace was built from 1735–40 under Freiherr von Neuhaus, Later the "Counts Preysing" had their second Town Palace here. The facade of the building reveals similarities to that of "Palais Holnstein", however the details come out rough rather than delicate and slender. The optical highlight are the rich and splendent colours of the facade.

Portia Palace

1694 the "Portia Palace" was built for the Fugger, the most famous banker family in Germany, by Zucalli as a Baroque Palace modelled on an Italian Palazzo.
Prince Elector Karl Albrecht commissioned his court architect Cuvilliés the Elder to reconfigure the building into rococo style, and made it as a present to his mistress Freiin Morawitzky, the later Countess Portia.

Prinz-Carl-Palais

Der heutige Sitz des Ministerpräsidenten von Bayern ging aus einem Adelspalast hervor: Als Stadtpalais Salabert – benannt nach dem Bauherrn Minister Abbé Pierre de Salabert – wurde er 1804/11 nach der Planung von Karl von Fischer am Zugang zum Englischen Garten erbaut. Später erwarb Prinz Carl das Gebäude. Der Name „Prinz-Carl-Palais" wurde aber erst im 20. Jahrhundert gebräuchlich.

Vor Ort

Nehmen Sie sich die Zeit, an einem Sonntagmorgen durch den Residenzgarten zu bummeln. Wenn Sie sich in östlicher Richtung bewegen, erreichen Sie bald die Staatskanzlei, ein Kuppelbau, flankiert von zwei gläsernen Seitenflügeln. Ein kleiner Weg führt Sie links den Hügel hinab zum leuchtend gelben Prinz-Carl-Palais. Im Gegensatz zu den reich verzierten barocken Palais besticht dieser Bau durch seine klassische Eleganz.

Informationen zur Geschichte und Architektur

Bereits wenige Jahre nach dem Bau kam es im Auftrag des neuen Besitzers Prinz Carl 1826/30 im Inneren des klassizistischen Palais zu Umgestaltungen. Später entstand der „Stallungs- und Dienst-Anbau" an der Von-der-Tann-Straße.

Im „Bautechnischen Führer durch München" von 1876 ist kritisch vermerkt: „Salons und Cabinete im Innern sind graziös aber so wenig für eine Familienwohnung berechnet", dass nach dem Tode Prinz Carls, als das Palais „an den Staat zurückfiel, dem Hauptgebäude ein Annex angefügt werden musste, um es durch Vermiethung (dermalen an den österreichischen Gesandten) nutzbar machen zu können". Mitte der 1870er Jahre wurde der „Dienst-Anbau" zum obersten Rechnungshof (im Erdgeschoss) und zur Dienstwohnung des Finanzministers umgebaut, dessen Ministerium nahebei, an der Ecke Galeriestraße/Ludwigstraße, stand.

Hitler plante dann eine Nutzung des Palastes als Gästehaus, das zuerst Mussolini anlässlich seines Besuches in München bewohnen sollte: 1937 erfolgten eine Erweiterung gen Westen, die Anpassung der Nord- an die Südfassade und ein Umbau des Inneren, wobei die Einfahrt zur Eingangshalle wurde.

Da das Palais den Zweiten Weltkrieg weitgehend unbeschädigt überstand, konnte die Staatliche Antikensammlung aus der Alten Pinakothek gerettete Exponate im Erdgeschoss unterbringen. 1948 bezog die Bayerische Akademie der Schönen Künste das Obergeschoss.

Seit den 1970er Jahren dient das Haus nun wieder als Sitz des Ministerpräsidenten.

Der zum Palais gehörige Finanzgarten entstand nach 1802 unter Einbeziehung von Resten der städtischen Wallbefestigung als Landschaftsgarten zwischen Hofgarten und Englischem Garten.

Information

Königinstr. 1, München
Verkehrsanbindung: U-Bahnlinien 3/4/5/6 bis Odeonsplatz.

Located at the northeast corner of the "Residence Garden" and at the southeast corner of the "English garden", as an architectural connection between them, is the "Prince Carl Palace". Arguably, it is the most precious and noble building of classicism in Munich.

Your Sightseeing

Stroll on a sunny Sunday morning between 8–10 o'clock through the Residence Garden. This gorgeous park gives you a relaxed, open-minded feeling. Go east towards the "Staatskanzlei" (characteristic building with its central classical dome and its two wings in modern glass-metal construction. Then turn left on the footpath downhill, and all of a sudden see the "Prince Carl Palace", its yellow colour glowing in the morning sunlight.

You will be rewarded with a unique impression: Compared to the Baroque and Rococo buildings, this Palace revels in aesthetic clearness. Compared to many of the massive, classical sights of Munich, it is elegant, appealing and luminous.

Circle around the Palace, explore its perspectives, and change your distance and viewing angles: this piece of architectural art shows off with different exciting characters.

Information about history and architecture

The "Town Palace Salabert" was built from 1804–1811 based upon the design from the renowned architect Karl v. Fischer, who modelled the building on the Italian garden villas of the Renaissance master builder Palladio.

On its main eastern front, the 2-storey Palace is characterised by a "Porticus" supported by colossal ionic pillars.

Already in 1826, the interior had been reconfigured for the new Owner, Prince Carl, brother of King Ludwig I.

Since the 1970s, the building is used for housing the most prominent guests of the Bavarian Prime Minister.

Prinz-Carl-Palais

Lenbach-Haus

Das Lenbach-Haus entstand als herrschaftlicher Sitz und Ateliergebäude des „Malerfürsten" Franz von Lenbach (1836–1904) in einer der damals vornehmsten Regionen der Stadt. Dies verdeutlicht den gesellschaftlichen Rang des Künstlers, der als der Porträtmaler im Deutschen Kaiserreich galt. Allein von Bismarck soll er etwa 80 Porträts geschaffen haben! Das Gebäude wird heute als städtische Galerie genutzt.

Vor Ort

Sie betreten den Garten der Villa durch ein schmiedeeisernes Tor und fühlen sich zwischen den Bäumen, Hecken, Statuen und dem dreistöckigen Brunnen aus Carrara-Marmor sogleich wie in Italien!
Im Inneren der Villa erwartet Sie eine exquisite Ausstellung mit Werken aus der Zeit der Romantik und des Biedermeier, die Hauptwerke der Künstlergruppe „Blauer Reiter" sowie moderne Kunst von Beuys, Warhol und anderen.

Informationen zur Geschichte und Architektur

Nach Plänen des bedeutenden und gefragten Architekten Gabriel von Seidl wurde das Lenbach-Haus 1887–91 in der Art einer italienischen „villa suburbana", einer toskanisch-römischen Vorstadtvilla, in Formen der Renaissance und des Barock erbaut. Es entstand eine geordnete, insgesamt jedoch malerische, asymmetrische Anlage mit einem auf den Garten ausgerichteten Wohnhaus und dem Atelierbau im Süden. 1927–29 kam der Nordflügel als Erweiterungsbau für das zwischenzeitlich eingerichtete Museum hinzu.
Im Zweiten Weltkrieg wurden die Bauten weitgehend zerstört, wobei der größte Teil der beachtlichen Innenausstattung verloren ging. Beim Neuaufbau 1954–58 wurde das Innere z. T. stark verändert, 1969/72 entstand der Anbau im Westen. Die nach den Kriegszerstörungen besser erhaltenen Teile des Mittelbaus erfuhren in den 1990er Jahren eine Renovierung, wobei man sich bemühte, dem Originalszustand möglichst nahe zu kommen, d. h. hier ist der Geist der Künstlervilla der Wilhelminischen Zeit zwischen Historismus und Jugendstil noch bzw. wieder spürbar.
Nicht wiederzugewinnen war der Ursprungszustand des ebenfalls im Krieg zerstörten Atelierbaus (Südflügel), in dem sich, außer dem Atelier, im ersten Obergeschoss einige prunkvoll ausgestattete Räume mit einer „Grotte" im Eingangsbereich befanden. Die Innenaufteilung war beim Neuaufbau teils abgeändert worden, doch wurden 1986 zur großen Franz-von-Lenbach-Ausstellung Räume rekonstruiert.
Erwähnenswert ist der dreistufige, vermutlich italienische Schalenbrunnen aus Carrara-Marmor (16./17. Jahrhundert) vor dem Haus. Die Figur des Knaben wurde später ergänzt.

Information

Städtische Galerie im Lenbachhaus und Kunstbau, Luisenstr. 33, München, Tel. 089-23332000, Fax 089-23332003/-04, Mail: lenbachhaus@muenchen.de, Internet www.lenbachhaus.de, Telefonansage: 089-23332002; geöffnet Di-So und feiertags 10-18 Uhr (Münchner Maler von der Gotik bis zur Gegenwart). Museumscafé Di-So 10-18 Uhr. Tel. 089-5237214. Museumsshop Di-So 10-18 Uhr. Tel. 089-525879.
Verkehrsanbindung: U-Bahnlinie 2 bis Königsplatz.

Very few steps northwest to the Königsplatz lies the "Villa Lenbach" ("Lenbach-Haus"), its architecture like a Tuscany suburban villa, a three-wing building enclosing a marvellous garden.
It was once owned by the famous portrait painter Franz von Lenbach and today is housing a spectacular exhibition of art paintings.

Your Sightseeing

You enter the villa's garden through the wrought iron garden gate. The best time is on a weekday or even better Sunday morning between 8–10 a.m.. Take time to linger in the garden for a while and to enjoy its Italianate layout with trees, hedges, statues and the 3-tiered shell fountain, made of Carrara marble stone.
Inside you will be rewarded with an extraordinary exhibition, confronting three epochs of paintings: from the 19th century Romanticism and Biedermeier style, the major works from the "Blue Rider" group Kandinsky, Marc and Macke, and paintings of modern art like from Beuys, Kubin, Warhol and others.

Information about history and architecture

According to the plans from the architect Gabriel v. Seidl, in 1891 the villa was built, modelled on Tuscan-Roman suburban villas, for Franz Lenbach. In Munich he was named the "Painter Prince", very popular as a portrait painter. Among his numerous clients have been persons like Emperor Wilhelm I, Prince Regent Luitpold, Habsburg Emperor Franz Joseph I and German chancellor Bismarck.
Therefore, Lenbach got wealthy enough, to own a villa having palatial dimensions.

Lenbach-Haus
mit Blick in die Inneräume

Villa Stuck

Der vom Bäckersohn aus Tettenweiß/Niederbayern zum „Malerfürsten" in der Hauptstadt München aufgestiegene Franz (von) Stuck (1863–1928), machte sich als Maler, Graphiker, Bildhauer und Plakatkünstler gleichermaßen einen Namen. Neben Franz von Lenbach war er der bedeutendste Salonmaler Münchens. Stuck gehörte zu den Begründern der Münchner Sezession, in der sich, in Abgrenzung zur damals vorherrschenden historisierenden Landschaftsmalerei, naturalistische, impressionistische und Jugendstiltendenzen mischten. 1895 wurde er Professor an der Akademie.
Die Villa Stuck liegt an der ab 1895 angelegten Prinzregentenstraße, einer Prachtstraße der vornehmen Vorstadt Bogenhausen und sollte die seines Konkurrenten Franz von Lenbach übertreffen.

Vor Ort

Da die Hauptfassade des Gebäudes gen Norden zeigt, bekommt sie nur in den frühen Morgenstunden einige Sonnenstrahlen ab, bietet dann aber einen atemberaubenden Anblick. Dieser Eindruck setzt sich beim Besuch der Innenräume fort, beherbergen sie doch die wichtigsten Werke des Jugendstils in ganz Deutschland. Unbedingt anschauen sollten Sie auch die Fresken und Gemälde des einstigen Hausherren im Untergeschoss.

Informationen zur Geschichte und Architektur

1897/98 entstand der monumentale Bau, zu dem Stuck selbst die Pläne lieferte. Auch Ausstattung und Dekoration wurden vom „Universalgenie" entworfen. Es entstand eine Künstlerresidenz des Jugendstils, ein Repräsentationsbau, der die potentielle Kundschaft beeindrucken und ein Treffpunkt der Münchner Gesellschaft werden sollte.
In einer zweiten Bauphase wurde der Atelierbau 1913/14, wiederum nach Entwürfen Stucks, hinzugefügt.
Nachdem die Villa im Zweiten Weltkrieg durch Brandbomben im Dachgeschoss beschädigt worden war, erfolgte nach dem Krieg eine weitgehende Wiederherstellung der Salons im Erdgeschoss sowie des Ateliers im ersten Obergeschoss, während andere Bereiche als Ausstellungsräume eingerichtet wurden.
1968 wurde das Museum (Prunkräume, Werke Stucks, Jugendstil-Gefäße) eröffnet, das sich seit 2005, nach einer 13-jährigen Restaurierungszeit, wieder in ganzer Pracht und Schönheit präsentiert.
Die Villa setzt sich aus zwei kubischen Baublöcken von monumentaler Wirkung, dem Atelierbau und dem Wohnhaus, zusammen. Beide sind, trotz der Jugendstil-Details, durch den Neoklassizismus geprägt. Als „Griechisches Haus" wurde die Villa (mit Eckrisaliten, Säulen-Portikus und flachem Dach) bezeichnet.
Die Innenräume gehören zum Eindrucksvollsten, was der symbolistische Jugendstil in Deutschland geschaffen hat. Dazu gehören mythologische Darstellungen und die für Stuck bezeichnenden Werke zu Eros und Musik. Die Villa ist insofern ein Gesamtkunstwerk der Architektur, Bildhauerei, Malerei und des Kunstgewerbes.

Information

Prinzregentenstr. 60, München, Tel. 089-45555125, Fax 089-45555124, geöffnet Mi-So 11-18 Uhr. Wechselausstellungen (Jugendstil, Klassische Moderne, angewandte Kunst, Kunst der Gegenwart).
Verkehrsanbindung: U-Bahnlinien 4/5 bis Max-Weber-Platz oder Prinzregentenplatz.

About 2 km east to town centre is located the "Villa Stuck", a total art work of architecture, sculptures, paintings and arts and crafts. The resplendent building is a unique combination of Neo-classical and Art Nouveau-style elements.

Your Sightseeing

Since the main front of the Villa is facing to the north, its facade is sunlit just the first hour after sunrise. At this time, the exterior of the building meets you with a breathtaking view.
You step inside and find rooms, which easily are amongst the most significant Art Nouveau-works in whole Germany. The ground floor shows up with frescoes and paintings from the owner Stuck himself. The first floor houses a permanent collection of exquisite Art Nouveau-pieces.

Information about history and architecture

Franz von Stuck was equally famous in Munich as Lenbach. He created paintings, graphic arts and sculptures as well, and he became professor at the Munich academy of arts.
His villa, which he wanted even to exceed the "Lenbach Villa", was built in 1897/98, and Stuck himself made the exterior and interior design.
The building is made up of two monumental cubic blocks, the studio and the private house. Front reliefs, pillars and a flat roof strongly contribute to the Greek style impression of the villa.

Villa Stuck

Asam-Schlössl

Im Jahre 1724 erwarb der aus einer bedeutenden oberbayerischen Künstlerfamilie stammende Maler und Baumeister Cosmas Damian Asam (1686–1739) ein seit 1687 bestehendes Landgut in Thalkirchen. Dessen Herrenhaus ließ er als Wohn- und Atelierhaus für sich umbauen, und 1729/30 schuf er selbst die Fassadenmalereien. Solche Malereien waren bis ins späte 18. Jahrhundert in München durchaus verbreitet, doch fielen die am Schlössl wegen ihrer aufwändigen Gestaltung aus dem Rahmen des Üblichen, denn C. D. Asam war in seinen illusionistischen Raum- und Wandgestaltungen stark durch den italienischen Maler und Baumeister Andrea Pozzo, den Meister der „unbegrenzten Perspektive", geprägt.

Vor Ort

Da sich das Gebäude in einer viel befahrenen Straße befindet, empfiehlt sich ein Besuch an einem ruhigen Sonntagmorgen. So kommen Sie in den ungestörten Genuss der reichen Fassadenmalerei. Außerdem empfiehlt sich ein Besuch des Restaurants im Schlössl, wo Sie die angebotenen bayerischen Spezialitäten in den Innenräumen oder im Gartenlokal einnehmen können.

Informationen zur Geschichte und Architektur

Zu Asams Landsitz gehörten außer dem Herrenhaus einige Nebengebäude, ein großer barocker Ziergarten sowie eine 1807 abgebrochene Kapelle. Wie die Kapelle wurden die meisten Nebengebäude des Schlössls im 19. Jahrhundert beseitigt. Ab 1838 diente das mit einem Anbau versehene Schlössl als Ausflugslokal. 1923-27, das Anwesen gehörte inzwischen der Stadt, wurde das baulich vernachlässigte Gebäude nach Planung des Architekten Hans Grässel instand gesetzt, die Fassadengemälde rekonstruiert.
Ein Bombenangriff 1944 legte das Gebäude in Schutt und Asche. Die Ruine wurde gesichert und 1958/59 als Wohnhaus wieder aufgebaut. Dabei wurden auch die Fassadenbilder erneuert.
Auf Darstellungen des Landgutes vor dem Ausbau unter Asam geht hervor, dass das Herrenhaus ein schlichter, zweistöckiger Bau mit Satteldach war. 1724 wurde es um ein weiteres Geschoss erhöht und erhielt dabei das hohe, den First des Satteldaches überragende Zwerchhaus mit großformatigen Rundbogenfenstern aufgesetzt; hierin befand sich Asams Atelier.

Information

Maria-Einsiedel-Str. 45, München
Verkehrsanbindung: U-Bahnlinie 3 bis Thalkirchen.

In a southern suburb of Munich named Thalkirchen lies the "Asam-Schlössl", once the country seat of Cosmas Damian Asam, a major painter of the baroque period. The main façade to the north as well as the southern garden side façade, are both covered with large magnificent wall paintings created by Asam himself.
Today the villa is housing a restaurant, well known for its regional cuisine.

Your Sightseeing

Since the villa is directly bordering a busy street, you should make your visit on a Sunday morning. In the very early hours, the red sun, reflecting in the windowpanes, is well harmonising with the rich colours of the façade paintings. At this daytime, you would have a singular view on the villa "Asam-Schlössl".
The rest of the morning you might stroll through the park, directly opposite to the villa. This is a fine spot for contemplation and recuperation, overmore at the northern end of the park you find another sight worth to see: an old pilgrimage church of the Baroque ages.
At noontime, do not miss to return to the "Asam-Schlössl" and to visit its popular restaurant. They offer Bavarian style dishes, which you have the option to enjoy either inside the restaurant or in the garden lounge.

Information about history and architecture

1729 the renowned painter and master builder Cosmas Damian Asam acquired a country seat in Thalkirchen near Munich. He commissioned the architect Schleich to rebuild the 2-tiered manor house into a three-storey villa, the façade paintings of which he added himself in 1729/30. Same year his brother Egid Quirin Asam built a house chapel northwest to the villa.

MARIA EINSIEDEL

Domburg/Residenz Freising

Auf dem die Stadt Freising, ca. 30 km nördlich von München, überragenden Berg nördlich der Isar steht der Dom des im Jahre 739 gegründeten Bistums Freising. Und im frühen 8. Jahrhundert stand hier eine Burg des Bayern-Herzogs aus dem Geschlecht der Agilofinger, zu der ein „palatium" (= Palast) und eine Marienkirche gehörten. Seit dem 11. Jahrhundert ist die Stadt am Fuß des Dom- und Burgberges bezeugt. Als Bischofssitz wurde die Burg bis ins 17. Jahrhundert mehrfach umgebaut.

Vor Ort

Auf Ihrem Weg von München nach Freising ist die Domburg weithin sichtbar. Eine kleine Straße mit Kopfsteinpflaster führt den Berg hinauf zur Burg und in eine andere Welt ... Sogleich nimmt einen die feierliche Atmosphäre alter Kirchen gefangen.

Der Dom selbst kann wegen mehrjähriger Renovierungsarbeiten nicht besucht werden. Sie können aber in die Krypta hinuntersteigen.

Versäumen Sie nicht, auch die Residenz zu besuchen. Das Renaissancegebäude mit seinen zweistöckigen Arkaden wird Sie ebenso begeistern wie der Rundblick, der sich Ihnen vom Berg aus bietet.

Informationen zur Geschichte und Architektur

Von 1519 datieren die Hofarkaden mit ihren Rippengewölben am Nord- und Ostflügel, ihre Rotmarmorsäulen schuf Stefan Rottaler aus Landshut. Im Inneren befinden sich mehrere sehenswerte Räume, insbesondere zwei wohl 1619 mit Stuck ausgestattete Säle im Untergeschoss und die Hauskapelle der Fürstbischöfe im Nordostturm (1617) mit beinahe vollplastischen Figuren Christi und der Evangelisten in der Kuppel sowie ein Altarretabel (= - aufsatz) von Philipp Dirr (1617/21). Die Decke im Vorraum der Kapelle wurde um 1715 von Nikolaus Liechtenfurtner stuckiert. Neben der Kapelle setzt der so genannte Fürstengang (1682) an, der die Residenz mit dem Dom verband und später mit Bildprogrammen ausgestattet wurde.

Im ersten Obergeschoss der Residenz liegen die Räume des Fürstbischofs, im zweiten ein prächtiger Saal mit Stuckausstattung von Johann Baptist Zimmermann (um 1715/20).

An Bischof Otto von Freising (1138–58), den Geschichtsschreiber und Onkel Kaiser Friedrichs I. Barbarossa, erinnert das Denkmal im Domhof von 1858.

Atop a hill, towering above Freising, an old medium size town 30 km north from Munich sits visible over a long distance, the "Dome Castle". The building complex encloses the "Cathedral" and the "Prince Bishop's Residence", the latter one of the earliest secular Renaissance buildings of ancient Germany.

Your Sightseeing

On an early afternoon, approaching Freising from Munich, you have a scenic view on the "Dome Castle" hill, which dominates the landscape from kilometres away.

In Freising you take the old small cobbled street uphill to the dome and after a few minutes you arrive in a different world: The "Dome Castle" welcomes you as a stately complex with the solemnity of ancient churches. The cathedral itself is under renovation for years, but you can step down into the crypt, a place always between daylight and darkness. You should go into the gothic "Johannis Church" and into the "Johannis Chapel". Visit the Residence, a grandiose Renaissance building and do not miss to walk along the 2-tiered arcade colonnades in the inner courtyards.

In the late afternoon sunlight and even more at sunset, you will be rewarded with a spectacular panorama view over the plain landscape, surrounding the dome hill.

Information about history and architecture

In the early eighth century, there were seated here a castle of the Bavarian Dukes, a palace and a "Church of our Lady".

The town Freising has been documented back as early as to the 11th century. The ancient Romanic dome was built around 1200, several expansions and reconfigurations transforming it into Gothic and baroque architectures took place up to the 17th century.

Domburg/Residenz Freising

Blick auf den Altar

Im Philipp-Schloss (Domberg 3-5), einer 1534-37 für Bischof Philipp von Bayern nach Plänen von Hans Reiffenstuel errichteten Vierflügelanlage, blieben im wesentlichen die Umfassungsmauern: Seit den 1980er Jahren dient das Schloss als Dom-Gymnasium. Eine zweischiffige Halle mit Säulen aus rotem Marmor und Fragmente von Wandmalereien sind im Inneren erhalten.

Information

Diözesanmuseum Freising, Domberg 21, Freising, Tel. 08161-48790, Fax 08161-487925. Große Teile des Dom- und Burgberges sind tagsüber frei zugänglich.
Verkehrsanbindung: S-Bahnlinie 1 bis Freising, von da ca. 10 Min. zu Fuß.

The central hall was decorated by the brothers Asam, the high altar adorned with the Rubens painting "Apocalyptic Maria".
The arcades of the Residence are dated from 1519, inside the building are two halls decorated with stuccoes from 1619. The first floor houses the rooms of the Prince Bishop, the second floor has a magnificent hall with stucco ornaments from Johann Baptist Zimmermann.

Blick in die Krypta

Arkaden der Domburg

Schloss Blutenburg

(München-Obermenzing)

Am Ostufer der Würm steht das stimmungsvolle Wasserschloss Blutenburg, das wesentlich auf Baumaßnahmen unter Herzog Albrecht III. in den 1430er Jahren und einen Umbau nach 1676 zurückgeht. Erst im 15. Jahrhundert urkundlich erwähnt, hatte es im 12./13. Jahrhundert einen Vorgängerbau: 1981 wurden im Herrenhaus Baureste eines Wohnturmes entdeckt.

Vor Ort

Blutenburg ist ein Gesamtkunstwerk aus mittelalterlicher Ritterburg, gotischer Kirche und Parkanlage und somit ein beliebtes Ausflugsziel für Familien. Neben der Internationalen Jugendbibliothek finden Sie im Inneren des Hauptgebäudes auch ein Erich-Kästner-Denkmal.

Informationen zur Geschichte und Architektur

Herzog Albrecht III., der die Burg mit seinen Frauen Agnes Bernauer (†1435) und Anna von Braunschweig bewohnte, bildete 1441 aus dem Dorf Menzing und der Burg die Herrschaft Menzing. Sein Sohn Sigismund verzichtete 1467 zugunsten seines jüngeren Bruders Albrecht IV. auf die Regierung, nahm Schloss Blutenburg als Wohnsitz und ließ ab 1488 die spätgotische Kirche in der Vorburg erbauen.

Durch die zunehmende Bedeutung von Schleißheim als Landsitz unter Wilhelm V. und Maximilian I. wurde Blutenburg ab dem Ende des 16. Jahrhunderts vernachlässigt. 1663 schenkte Kurfürst Ferdinand Maria die Herrschaft und den Weiler Kemnaten der Kurfürstin Henriette Adelaide. Ihr folgte der Notar Anton von Berchem als Besitzer von Herrschaft und Burg, die er zum Landsitz umbauen ließ.

Die bayerische Herrscherfamilie übernahm das Schloss im 19. Jahrhundert. 1979/83 erfolgte eine grundlegende Renovierung der Burg für die neue Nutzung als „Internationale Jugendbibliothek“. Hierfür wurde ein Teil des Burghofes unterkellert.

Die Hauptburg ist als mehreckige, mit vier Flankierungstürmen versehene Kastellburg konzipiert. Aus dem Wohnturm ging das mehrfach erweiterte Herrenhaus hervor.

Kunstgeschichtlich bedeutend ist die ab 1488 erbaute spätgotische Schlosskirche in der Vorburg, ein Saalbau mit Netzrippengewölbe, der 1856 auf Initiative von Karl Maria von Aretin (dem Begründer des Bayerischen Nationalmuseums) unter Verwendung originaler Teile „regotisiert“ wurde. Besonders bemerkenswert sind die Ausstattung und das Altartriptychon der Kirche.

Information

Seldweg 15, München-Obermenzing. Internationale Jugendbibliothek, Tel. 089-8912110.
Michael-Ende-Museum; geöffnet Sa-So 14-17 Uhr.
Schlosskapelle, Pfarramt „Leiden Christi“, Tel. 089-8911410; geöffnet Mo-Fr 7.30-17 Uhr, Sa, So, feiertags 9.30-17 Uhr.
Schlossschänke, Tel. 089-8119808; geöffnet 11-24 Uhr.
Verkehrsanbindung: S-Bahnlinien 4/5/6/8/20 bis Pasing und Buslinie 73/76 bis zum Schloss Blutenburg.

Situated at the east bank of the river Würm, on the western perimeter of Munich, is the late Gothic "Blutenburg Castle". Built as a hunting castle by the Wittelsbach Duke Albrecht III in the mid 15th century, it still looks like a romantic medieval knight's castle.
Today the "Blutenburg Palace" houses the "International Youth Library".

Your Sightseeing

The "Blutenburg Castle" offers an all-round sightseeing event. Not only the medieval knight´s castle itself, but also the park, the small lake in front of the castle, dotted with swans and other waterfowls, and the restaurant at the lake side will entertain you and your family.
The inner yard of the castle is dominated by a beautiful garden and a Gothic church in the centre, and you should not miss to see the art masterpieces in it.
Inside the main house and the gate tower, you will find the "Erich-Kästner-Memorial" and the international youth library.

Information about history and architecture

The main castle was constructed as a fort with four flanking turrets in 1430 under Duke Albrecht III, who lived here with Agnes Bernauer, a daughter from a low class family. From 1467 on his heir “Duke Sigismund“, after his renunciation of the throne, decided to live in the castle. He had built the late Gothic church in 1488, which he died in 14 years later.
The increasing importance of the "Schleißheim Palace" for the royal family in the 17th century very much reduced the role of "Blutenburg Castle".

Schloss Blutenburg

Schloss Dachau

Nachdem Konrad III., der letzte Graf von Dachau, 1182 gestorben war, fiel seine Grafschaft – und damit die Burg Dachau auf dem Felsen über dem Flüsschen Amper – an die Wittelsbacher. In der Renaissance- und Barockzeit entstand anstelle der Burg das prächtige Schloss mit einer der bedeutendsten Kassettendecken Deutschlands (16. Jahrhundert) und einem Garten, der zu den schönsten Gärten Bayerns gezählt wurde. Wohl nicht zuletzt deswegen, weil vom Dachauer Schlossberg aus die Residenzstadt München und ein großer Teil des Herzogtums Bayern zu überblicken waren, entwickelte sich das Schloss zum beliebten Aufenthaltsort des Münchner Hofes.

Vor Ort

Drei Dinge seien dem gestressten Besucher besonders empfohlen: Ein Spaziergang entlang des 300 Jahre alten Linden-Laubengangs, die Einkehr im Restaurant vor Ort, von dessen Veranda man einen herrlichen Blick in den Obstgarten hat, sowie der Rundblick auf München, der sich einem vom Felsen aus eröffnet. Die übrigen Sehenswürdigkeiten werden Ihnen ohnehin nicht entgehen ...

Informationen zur Geschichte und Architektur

Begonnen 1546 unter Herzog Wilhelm IV., wurde Schloss Dachau unter Herzog Albrecht V. als Renaissance-Vierflügelanlage vollendet. Zwar wurde sie später verändert und 1806/09 größtenteils abgebrochen, doch vermittelt der Festsaal seit 1979 wieder einen Eindruck frühneuzeitlicher Raumkunst: Die vom „Kistler" (= Schreiner) Hans Wisreutter aus München 1564–66 geschaffene hölzerne Prunk-Kassettendecke zieren Wappen der aus dem Hause Wittelsbach stammenden Schlossbauherren und ihrer Frauen, gruppiert um das Wappen Kaiser Ludwigs IV. des Bayern (1282–1347). Die heutige Anordnung entspricht nicht dem Original.

Zur Saal-Ausstattung gehörten ein Fußboden aus Kalk und Marmor, gläserne Wappenscheiben, der gemalte Götterfries und 13 Wandteppiche mit Darstellungen aus der Herkules-Sage von Michel de Bos. An die Stelle der Wandteppiche, die 1610 in die Residenz verbracht worden waren, trat später eine Porträtgalerie des Hauses Wittelsbach und seiner Verwandten.

1715–17 wurde der Saalflügel für Kurfürst Max Emanuel in der Art des französischen Spätbarocks umgebaut. Nach dem Teilabbruch des Schlosses 1806/09 blieb nur der Saalflügel erhalten. Wegen seiner Nutzung als Lagerhaus wurde die Kassettendecke 1868 ins Bayerische Nationalmuseum gebracht. Erst seit 1979 ist sie wieder am Originalort zu bewundern.

Sehenswert ist nach wie vor der mehrfach umgestaltete Schlossgarten mit seinem fast 300 Jahre alten Linden-Laubengang.

Information

Schlossstr. 7, Dachau, Tel. 08131-87923; Auskunft: Schloss- und Gartenverwaltung Schleißheim-Dachau, Tel. 089-3158720, Fax 089-31587250; geöffnet Di-So, April-Sept. 9-18 Uhr, Okt.-März 10-16 Uhr (für Gehbehinderte gibt es eine Rampe, außerdem einen Aufzug). Das Schloss-Café lädt zum Verweilen ein.

Verkehrsanbindung:
S-Bahnlinie 2 bis Dachau und Buslinie 720 bis Rathaus.

"Dachau Castle" is located atop a hill, 500 metres above the town of Dachau.
The magnificent building from Renaissance and Baroque ages arguably has one of the most adorable palace gardens in Bavaria.

Your Sightseeing

When you visit "Dachau Castle", you would like to enjoy three things. You stroll around in the palace garden under the 300 years old linden trees, you dine inside the restaurant or on the south veranda, looking at the orchard, and you have the panorama view over Munich.
On a weekday afternoon you will be rewarded by the best sunlight conditions.

Information about history and architecture

The construction was started in 1546 under Duke Wilhelm IV Duke Albrecht V had the building completed in 1573. It came out as a 4-wing Renaissance building complex with 108 rooms and 350 windows, and centred around a courtyard.
Between 1715–17 Prince Elector Max Emanuel II commissioned his court architect Joseph Effner to reconfigure the great hall modelled on late French Baroque.
1806, after the severe damaging by Napoleon's troops, King Max Joseph I had torn down three of the four wings. The one wing containing the great hall is what has been left today.

Schloss Dachau

Blick auf Schloss Dachau von der Gartenseite

Burg Grünwald

Über dem östlichen Steilufer der Isar erhebt sich eindrucksvoll die Burg Grünwald, die an der Stelle römischer Baureste stehen soll.
Herzog Ludwig der Strenge erwarb 1293 Besitzungen Ulrichs von Vellenberg, eines Ministerialen der Grafen von Andechs, und erbaute hier die Burg Grünwald.

Vor Ort

Grünwald ist ein schicker, ruhiger Ort, etwa 10 km südlich des Stadtkerns von München. Ein Besuch der Burg führt Sie direkt in die Vergangenheit zurück, hat sie doch bis heute nichts von ihrem mittelalterlichen Charakter verloren. Gehen Sie auf Entdeckunsgreise und erkunden auch das Innere des Gebäudes mit seinem mächtigen Turm.

Informationen zur Geschichte und Architektur

1319-1490 war Grünwald Sitz der Jägermeister von Oberbayern, denn bis ins 16. Jahrhundert war die Region ein beliebtes Jagdgebiet der Herzöge von Bayern. Noch 1486/87 kam es zu einem Umbau der Burg, die damals im Wesentlichen ihr jetziges Erscheinungsbild erhielt.
Wilhelm IV. und Ludwig X. beschlossen hier im Februar 1522 während der „Grünwalder Konferenz" eine gegen Luthers Reformation gerichtete Religionspolitik.
Bei einer Versteigerung erwarb 1879 der Münchner Bildhauer und Präparator Paul Zeiller die Burg und ließ sie im Sinne des Historismus zum Wohnbau umgestalten.
Schließlich übernahm 1977 der Freistaat Bayern die Anlage und brachte dort eine Zweigstelle der Prähistorischen Staatssammlung München unter.
Trotz aller Abbrüche und Umbauten vermittelt Burg Grünwald noch viel vom spätgotischen Erscheinungsbild am Ende des 15. Jahrhunderts. Selbst Reste der Wall-Graben-Befestigung sind an der Ost- und Nordseite noch erkennbar. Die Burg hat einen unregelmäßigen, einem Rechteck angenäherten Grundriss. Zur letzten mittelalterlichen Bauphase gehört der Torbau, der am Stufengiebel Wappen von Herzögen und ihren Gattinnen zeigt. Auch die Ecktürme stammen in heutiger Form aus jener Bauphase, ebenso der Rundturm des Zwingers und der Westflügel mit dem kleinen Turm.

Information

Burgmuseum Grünwald, Zweigmuseum der Prähistorischen Staatssammlung, Zeillerstr. 3, Grünwald, Tel. 089-64113218; geöffnet 15.3.-30.11. Mi-So 10-16.30 Uhr; Gruppenführung Tel. 089-2112402.
Verkehrsanbindung: S-Bahnlinie 25 bis Grünwald.

In the suburb Grünwald, about 10 km south of Munich centre, is "Grünwald Castle". Seated on the steep east bank of the Isar river, the gothic knight's castle has fully retained its medieval character.

Your Sightseeing

In the midst of a sunny morning, Grünwald is a fashionable calm village also on weekday, the sun lights up the bright façades and wall exteriors of the romantic building. Enjoy to circle around or to step inside, always will the mighty tower, the long wall and the gate painted with several ducal coats of arms give a delightful perspective. Today the castle houses parts of the "Bavarian State Prehistoric Collection".

Information about history and architecture

In 1293 Duke Ludwig the Stringent acquired a piece of land and had built a castle named "Gruoninwalde". A reconstruction of the castle was done in 1486/87, and this late Gothic architecture still today characterises the castle.
The ground plan, albeit somewhat irregular, is approximately rectangular. Four corner towers and a round ward are the most significant architectural elements.

Burg Grünwald

„Burg“ Schwaneck

(Pullach im Isartal)

Am Steilufer westlich der Isar erhebt sich die „Burg“ Schwaneck – keine mittelalterliche Burg, sondern der romantische Wohnsitz des zur Zeit König Ludwigs I. prominenten Bildhauers Ludwig Schwanthaler (1802–1848).

Vor Ort

Nachmittags lädt die Auenlandschaft im Isartal, die die Burg umgibt, zum Verweilen ein. Der Turm der Burg ist nun in das schönste Licht getaucht. Machen Sie einen Spaziergang über den Burghof und lassen sich gedanklich in längst vergangene Zeiten entführen.

Informationen zur Geschichte und Architektur

Schwaneck ist ein Produkt der Mittelalterbegeisterung des 19. Jahrhunderts, die nicht bloß Schwärmerei war, sondern im Mittelalter das Vorbild für die eigene Zeit sah. Friedrich von Gärtner lieferte die aus finanziellen Gründen nur sehr reduziert umgesetzten Pläne zur Burg, die, 1840/42 erbaut, mit einer „Erstürmung“ 1843 eingeweiht wurde. Der Bauherr selbst hatte Entwürfe vorgegeben und Skizzen geliefert. Wie sehr der Bau mit künstlerischen Ideen verflochten war, zeigt auch die Tatsache, dass eine fiktive Burg Schwaneck an der Isar der Schauplatz einer Zauber-Oper war, welche die von Schwanthaler gegründete Künstlervereinigung der „Humpenauer“ aufführte.

Die Ursprungsbauten bilden der 26 m hohe Wohnturm mit Zinnenkranz und achteckigem Treppenturm, der Pförtnerbau und die Ringmauer mit Zugbrücke. Zum Raumprogramm des Turmes gehörte neben Wohn- und Schlafräumen der Rittersaal mit Kapellenerker und Balkon im obersten Stock.

Schwanthalers Vetter Franz Xaver Schwanthaler, er war ebenfalls Bildhauer, und dessen Kinder Rudolf und Sophie verkauften Schwaneck 1863 an Dr. Karl Mayr Ritter von Mayrfels (†1883), einen bekannten Heraldiker (= Wappenforscher), Altertumsforscher, Kunst- und „Burgensammler“ aus München. Ihm gehörten auch das Alte Schloss in Meersburg/Bodensee und zeitweise einige Burgen in Südtirol. Der neue Besitzer ließ Schwaneck umgestalten und erweitern. So entstanden ein neuer Flügel mit der Kapelle St. Hubertus, ein Rundturm und eine Trinkhalle nordwestlich des Wohnturmes.

Jakob Heilmann (†1927), der führende Bauunternehmer in München, erwarb Schwaneck 1899 und ließ die Burg 1900/02 als Landsitz ausbauen. Die Trinkhalle wurde damals durch einen neuen Rittersaal mit offenem Dachstuhl ersetzt. Die Neubauten an der Süd- und Südostseite des Hofes weisen Elemente von Historismus, Jugendstil und Heimatschutz auf, sie repräsentieren den Stilpluralismus der Wilhelminischen Zeit, insbesondere in den Räumen des ersten Obergeschosses.

Nachdem der Landkreis München die „Burg“ 1955 erworben hatte, überließ er sie dem Kreisjugendring als Geschäfts- und Schulungsstelle und Jugendherberge. 1973–75 wurde das Anwesen um einen so genannten angepassten Neubau erweitert.

Information

Jugendherberge Burg Schwaneck, Kreisjugendring München-Land, Burgweg 4, Pullach im Isartal, Tel. 089-74486670.
Verkehrsanbindung: S-Bahnlinie 7 bis Pullach.

Located on the west bank of river Isar, just a few kilometres north from Grünwald, is "Schwaneck Castle". It looks very much like a medieval knight´s castle, but it is not one. "Schwaneck Castle" is a creation from the romantic age in the early 19th century. Today it is house for a hostel.

Your Sightseeing

Around noontime, a weekend day is preferable, you enjoy the meadows of the quiet Isar valley, which are surrounding the castle's building complex. Now the sunlight is bright enough, to come through the dense leafy canopy of the trees, encircling the one tower. You would like to linger in the yard and to let your thoughts wander over the past.

Information about history and architecture

"Schwaneck Castle" was built in 1843 as a romantic building, which was at that time not only very popular to do, but has been the expression of a recollection, even an enthusiasm to medieval ages and culture. The initial building was the tower, 26 m high and made up of living rooms and the knights hall. The later constructed buildings reveal the architectural styles of Historicism and Art Nouveau in parallel.

„Burg Schwaneck“

Hofmarkschloss Planegg

Am westlichen Stadtrand von München in der Gemeinde Planegg steht das Hofmarkschloss, ein Renaissanceschloss mit barocker Fassade, umgeben von Wasser und einer Parkanlage im englischen Stil.

Vor Ort

Wir empfehlen Ihnen einen Tagesausflug von München nach Planegg. Am besten wählen Sie für Ihren Besuch die frühen Vormittagsstunden, dann erstrahlen Schloss und Park im schönsten Morgenlicht. Genießen Sie die Ruhe im Park um diese Zeit und die herrschaftliche Atmosphäre, die die Gebäude ausstrahlen. Die Innenräume des Schlosses sind nicht zugänglich.

Informationen zur Geschichte und Architektur

Der Wittelsbacher Herzog Wilhelm III. erwarb 1409 den Grund und Boden und ließ darauf für seinen illegitimen Sohn Konrad von Eggenhofen das Schloss bauen. 1550 wurde es als Renaissanceschloss errichtet, 1740 aber im Stil des Barock umgestaltet.

Nachdem das Dorf Planegg, das Schloss und das umgebende Land 1420 zur Hofgemarkung erklärt worden waren, konnten sich auch die privaten Landbesitzer Hofmarkherren und -richter nennen und durften Recht sprechen. Sie waren das Bindeglied zwischen den Grafen, Herzögen und Prinzen auf der einen und den Bauern, Arbeitern und Händlern auf der anderen Seite.

Information

Pasinger Straße 5, Planegg

Verkehrsanbindung: S-Bahnlinie 6 bis Planegg oder U-Bahnlinie 3 bis Fürstenried, dann Buslinie 260 bis Planegg.

On the western outskirts of Munich, in the centre of the small village Planegg is the "Homarkschloss Planegg". The Renaissance castle with its front exterior in baroque style is surrounded by water, seated in a large English-style park, and flanked by a separated court building.

Your Sightseeing

In the midst of the morning, you will find the best light to bring out the outline and shapes of the building and the garden as well. Make a stroll of it to circle around the area of the castle and the park and you might catch the mixture between scenic quietness and respectful manor and courthouse. This is what a "Court March Castle" was supposed to be.

Information about history and architecture

1409 the Wittelsbach Duke Wilhelm III acquired a large farm land and had built a castle on it for his illegitimate son Konrad von Eggenhofen. In 1550 the castle had been reconstructed into Renaissance style and 1740 into Baroque style architecture. Since 1420 the castle, the village Planegg and the surrounding land was declared as "Court March". The meanwhile private owners were announced "Court March Lords and Judges". They had the right to run the court march and to do the jurisdiction. They were the connecting link between the counts, dukes and princes on the noble side and the peasants, workmen and merchants on the lower class side.

Hofmarkschloss Planegg

Stadtresidenz Preysing
(Erding)

Erding, etwa 30 km nordöstlich von München gelegen, ist eine typisch bayerische Kleinstadt: sauber und ordentlich, malerisch und rustikal.
Die Stadt hat einen wunderschönen Marktplatz, dessen Nordseite von der Stadtresidenz Preysing flankiert wird.
Durch die Jahrhunderte war das Gebäude im Besitz verschiedener Adelsfamilien. Schließlich wurde daraus das prachtvolle Rathaus der Stadt.

Vor Ort

Für Ihren Besuch in Erding empfehlen wir einen Wochentag, es sein denn, Sie möchten auch das Städtische Heimatmuseum besuchen, das ist nur sonntagnachmittags möglich. Wochentags finden Sie allerdings das Rathaus geöffnet und sollten einen Rundgang durch das Innere unternehmen. Schließen Sie am besten einen Spaziergang durch Erding an und erkunden das lebhafte, hübsche Städtchen.

Informationen zur Geschichte und Architektur

Baron Johann Warmund von Preysing ließ im frühen 17. Jahrhundert die Residenz erbauen, die bereits im 30-jährigen Krieg (1618–48) zerstört wurde. Der Sohn des Grafen, Johann Bernhard Preysing, ließ das Gebäude später rekonstruieren. Es wurde hauptsächlich während der Jagdsaison als Gästehaus für den Kurfürsten genutzt.
Ende des 18. Jahrhunderts erwarben die Grafen von Seinsheim das Haus und bewohnten es bis 1797. Es folgten einige private Besitzer, bis es schließlich ab 1866 als Rathaus genutzt wurde.
Die Fassade wurde 1912 renoviert und mit wunderbaren Wandmalereien versehen, die die Wappen der ehemaligen adligen Besitzer zeigen.

Information

Landshuter Straße 1, Erding
Städtisches Heimatmuseum, Prielmayerstraße 1, Erding, Tel. 08122-187533, Öffnungszeiten: So 14.00–17. 00 Uhr.
Verkehrsanbindung: S-Bahnlinie 6 bis Erding.

Erding is a small town about 30 km north from Munich. It shows off with the typical character of Bavarian locations: clean, scenic and country style. This town has a beautiful market place, the north side of which is dominated by the "Town Residence Preysing". Over the years, this Baroque building was owned in succession by several count families. Finally, it became a marvellous city hall.

Your Sightseeing

You arrive preferably in the midst of a weekday morning. You find a good sunlight for viewing at a resplendent building. Do not miss to step inside and to visit the town's historical museum. After having explored the building, do not be sparing with your time, to explore this vivid and attractive little town.

Information about history and architecture

The Residence was built in the early 17th century by Baron Johann Warmund von Preysing, however it has been destroyed during the 30-years-war. The son of the baron, Count Johann Bernhard von Preysing had the building reconstructed, and mainly used it as an accommodate guesthouse for the prince elector during the hunting season. End of the 18th century, the building was acquired by the Counts von Seinsheim, who lived there until 1797. After having seen some private owners, from 1866 on it was used as the town hall. In 1912 the façade was renovated and adorned with magnificent wall paintings, depicting the coats of arms of the former noble owners.

Stadtresidenz Preysin

Weitere Bücher aus dem Wartberg Verlag über München

Elisabeth Angermair
München – Bewegte Zeiten – Die 50er Jahre
64 S., geb., zahlr. S/w-Fotos
Großformat
(ISBN 3-8313-1271-0)

Heidi und Georg Fruhstorfer
Hurra, wir leben noch! München nach 1945
64 S., geb., zahlr. S/w-Fotos
Großformat
(ISBN 3-8313-1336-9)

Rudi Dix und Heinz Gebhardt
Kindheit in München in den 50er Jahren
64 S., geb., zahlr. S/w-Fotos
Großformat
(ISBN 3-86134-396-7)

Dieter Grossherr (Hg.)
Das Millionendorf Münchner Geschichten aus den 50er Jahren
80 S., geb., zahlr. S/w-Fotos
(ISBN 3-8313-1142-0)

Heidi Fruhstorfer
Wir Kriegskinder – Münchner Zeitzeugen erinnern sich
64 S., geb., zahlr. S/w-Fotos
Großformat
(ISBN 3-8313-1488-8)

Uta Poss und Oscar Poss
Unsere Kindheit in Bayern in den 50er und 60er Jahren Von sauberen Madl und schneidigen Buam
64 S., geb., zahlr. S/w-Fotos
(ISBN 3-8313-1374-1)

Wartberg Verlag GmbH & Co. KG
Im Wiesental 1 • 34281 Gudensberg-Gleichen • Tel.: 0 56 03/9 30 50 • Fax: 0 56 03/30 83 • www.wartberg-verlag.de